…ition devised and selected by Tim … Southampton City Art Gallery. The … ibition is due to his dedication and energy. Its title, which has been with the project almost from its inception, is taken from an essay of 1910 by Walter Sickert about the Fitzroy Street Group, to which Gilman and Ratcliffe belonged: he wrote of their applying paint "with a clean and solid mosaic of thick paint in a light key", a description that captures very well the appeal of these artists' work.

The exhibition and this book explore the artistic development and relationship of Harold Gilman and his protégé William Ratcliffe, both founder members of the famous Camden Town Group, which succeeded the Fitzroy Street Group. They illustrate the development of Gilman's style from his early domestic interiors redolent of Manet and Velázquez to his 'full-blown' Post-Impressionist maturity, which evolved from his discovery of Van Gogh. Gilman was arguably the most talented painter in the Group led by Sickert and he exercised a substantial influence on Ratcliffe, who he met in Letchworth in 1908.

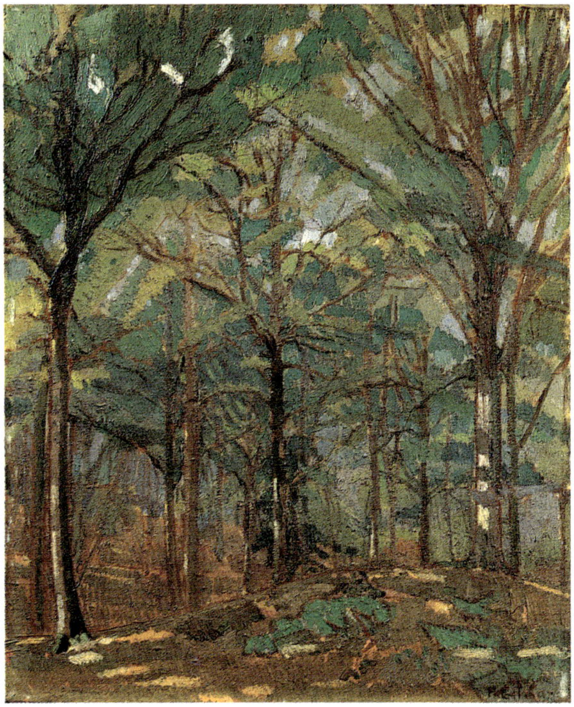

HAROLD GILMAN
Beech Wood, Gloucestershire, 1916
Oil on canvas, 624 x 508 mm
York City Art Gallery

William Ratcliffe is usually relegated to a minor role in the story of the Camden Town Group. This exhibition traces his close artistic relationship with Gilman and demonstrates that his painting was of comparable stature to his colleagues'.

Many public and private collections across England have generously lent paintings and drawings to the exhibition to augment the Gallery's own holdings. We would like particularly to thank all the lenders, both public and private, and especially Tate, London, and Ros Allwood of the Letchworth Museum and Art Gallery. Both Tim Craven and I would further like to thank Barbara Duce for the valuable information she has contributed to his essay. We are also grateful for the enthusiasm of Martin Brunt, who contributed to the exhibition at its early stages, and for the hard work of many others both inside and outside the Gallery.

ESTA MION-JONES

Letchworth

In 1911 Harold Gilman and William Ratcliffe became founder members of the Camden Town Group, an avant-garde exhibiting society of sixteen artists which evolved its ideas and impetus from French Post-Impressionism. Gilman, arguably the most gifted painter of the group, and Ratcliffe, his protégé, one of its more obscure members, enjoyed a fruitful relationship which flourished amidst the melting-pot of the prevalent radical art politics. This exhibition traces Gilman and Ratcliffe's development as artists, recording their gradual absorption of French and peer influence, and the progression of Ratcliffe's art both by Gilman's example and after his colleague's premature death in 1919.

Although it lasted only three years, holding a mere three exhibitions, the impact of the Camden Town Group on the development of British twentieth-century modernism proved substantial. The group came into existence when a small number of young, progressive artists, led by the London Impressionist Walter Sickert and by Lucien Pissarro, son of the famous French Impressionist Camille Pissarro, decided in desperation to found their own exhibiting society. The venues where traditionally professional artists needed to promote and sell their work if they were to become seriously and critically established – the Royal Academy and the recently founded New English Art Club – had slammed their doors against modern French art and reviled anything associated with it. The name 'Camden Town Group' was chosen by Sickert, who suggested that "... the district had been so watered with his tears that something important must sooner or later spring from its soil".[1]

The Group's common subject-matter and purpose were the objective recording of everyday urban life, often low life, both inside and out of doors. As Sickert described it in 1910, "The more our art is serious, the more will it tend to avoid the drawing-room and stick to the kitchen. The plastic arts are gross arts, dealing joyously with gross material facts ... and while they will flourish in the scullery, or the dunghill, they fade at the breath from the drawing-room."[2]

The story of the Camden Town Group is for the most part centred geographically around north London, but the Gilman–Ratcliffe relationship also involved two very different locations: Letchworth, situated 35 miles north of London in Hertfordshire, and Scandinavia. Today Letchworth might seem an unlikely place for two progressive artists to encounter one another, but in 1908 it was not so surprising. Then just five years old, Letchworth was the "the world's first garden city". It was the brainchild of Ebenezer

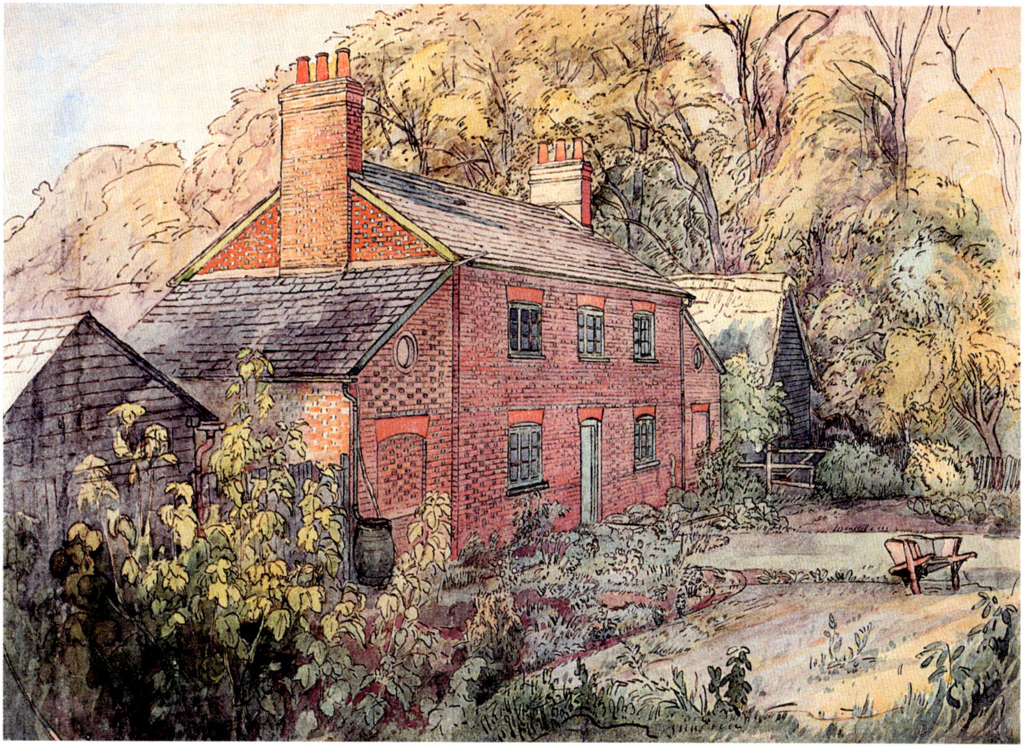

WILLIAM RATCLIFFE
Lower Wilbury Farm, c. 1930s
Watercolour, 380 x 536 mm
Letchworth Museum and Art Gallery

Howard (1850–1928), a Parliamentary reporter who had studied early industrial communities, including Cadbury's Bourneville of 1895. Combining their disparate elements into a new concept which expressed complex ideas with a disarming simplicity, he published *Tomorrow: A Peaceful Path to Real Reform* in 1898, re-issued in 1902 as *Garden Cities of Tomorrow*. Letchworth was a reaction against the Industrial Revolution and its legacy of grime and pollution, slum housing conditions and miserable poverty. To the founders it was a much needed attempt to integrate town with country and, by careful planning, to combine both rural space and urban amenities – a self-contained semi-paradise offering employment to all its inhabitants. The chief architects were Barry Parker and Raymond Unwin, whose red-and-white 'cottage style' gave Letchworth uniformity of design and its unique character.

Although Letchworth was not the first attempt to provide healthy working and living conditions for a working population, it was the first such settlement large enough to deserve the title 'city'. Its location was decided by the relatively cheap cost of Letchworth's poor-grade agricultural land, its timely availability and its proximity to London. The experiment proved a success, and suburban copies of Letchworth can now be seen throughout Britain. Indeed the vision was attractive. It offered the opportunity to enjoy improved living conditions in bright homes with gardens at low rents, rates and prices, amid the beauty of nature, pure air and pure water – and, above all, freedom and co-operation.[3] Letchworth naturally became a magnet for those of a free-thinking, progressive and socialist outlook, including artists, and it soon established a reputation among traditional towns and villages in the neighbourhood for harbouring Bohemian and strange types, despite the fact that there were strictly no pubs allowed there.

When Gilman moved into no. 15, Westholm Green, a terrace of cottages built by Parker and Unwin in 1908, Ratcliffe was already living a few doors down at no. 10, and their mutual interest soon brought them together.

William Ratcliffe

William Ratcliffe was born in October 1870 at Churchwater near King's Lynn. The family then moved to Manchester, where his father worked in a mill, but owing to their reduced circumstances both Ratcliffe's brother (S.K. Ratcliffe, later a *Manchester Guardian* journalist and lecturer) and his sister were sent to live with different relatives. While earning his living in a cotton merchant's office, for seven years he spent his evenings studying under the celebrated artist Walter Crane at Manchester School of Art, and it was Crane who instilled the methodical and disciplined approach to his work which remained with him throughout his life.

In 1894 Ratcliffe moved to London and for twelve years worked as a pattern designer for the Wallpaper Combine. Drawn by the exciting ideology that the fledgling garden city represented, he moved to Letchworth in 1906, to work, most probably, with one of the new printing companies, the Garden City Press Ltd. Certainly he produced art work for the official engagement calendar of the city and a series of postcard views of it. A neighbour of Ratcliffe's at Westholm Green was Stanley Parker, brother of the architect Barry, an art teacher. He taught Ratcliffe wood engraving and the two became lifelong friends.

Harold Gilman

Harold Gilman was born in 1876 at Rode in Somerset, where his father was a country parson. While at school in Tonbridge he suffered a severe injury to his hip, and during a protracted convalescence of eighteen months he discovered an aptitude for art. Following one year as a non-collegiate student at Oxford and another as tutor to English children in Odessa on the Black Sea, he eventually found his way to art school in Hastings. From there he

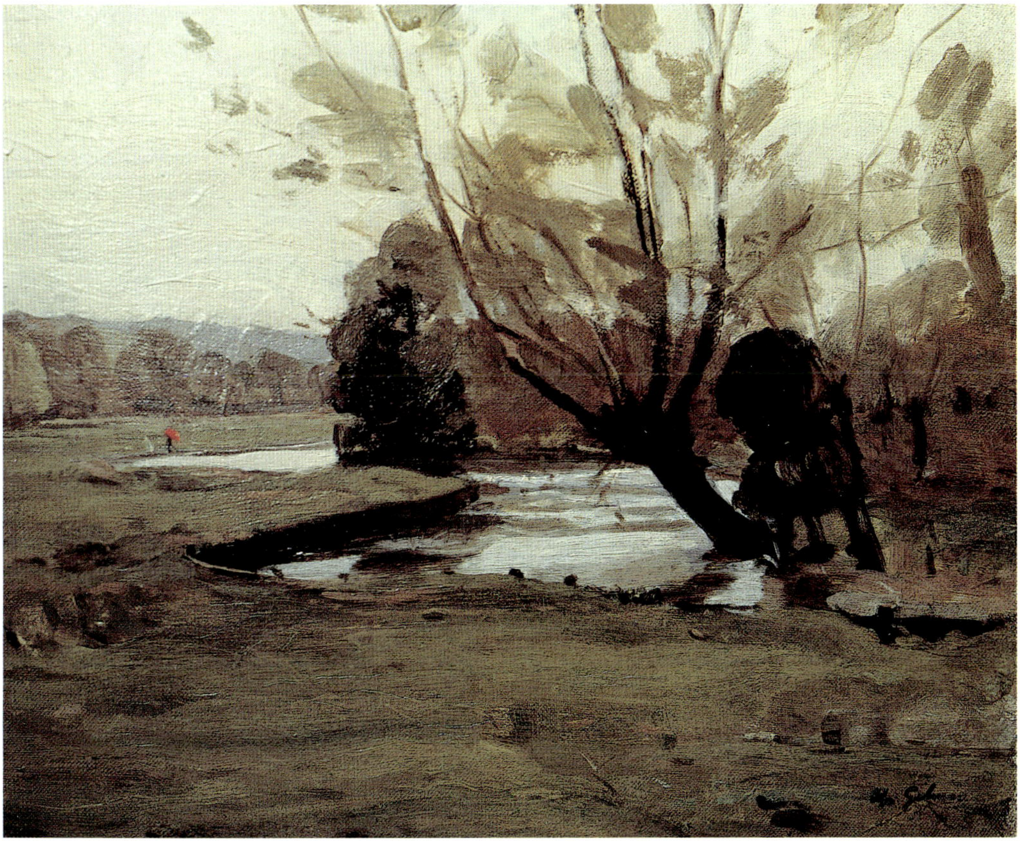

HAROLD GILMAN
Willows by a River, before 1905
Oil on canvas, 327 x 376 mm
Private collection

entered the celebrated Slade School of Art in London, where he remained until 1901, absorbing the sound teachings of the famously formidable Henry Tonks. Gilman then continued his studies for a further year at the Prado in Madrid, where he concentrated on making copies after Velázquez. This proved a very solid basis for his future career. His early painting bears the influence both of Whistler and of Velázquez's accurate and sensitive handling of tonal values.

While in Spain Gilman met and married an American artist, Grace Canedy, and their first daughter Elizabeth was born back in London in 1904. During this year his work was accepted for exhibition with the New English Art Club. Originally formed in 1888 by artists interested in French Impressionism who had been rejected by the Royal Academy, the NEAC soon lost its radical edge and became staid and complacent. Only two members, Philip Wilson Steer and Walter Sickert, could genuinely assume the title of Impressionist; the majority tended to produce saleable and tame pastiches of the movement as exemplified in France by the work of Jules Bastien-Lepage.

Gilman's early work was small in scale, domestic and intimate in subject-matter, and cool and sombre in colour. Tonal values predominate, laid on with thin, fluid and elegant brushwork. Quality of finish is immediately apparent in these paintings, for Gilman was a perfectionist and he continued to care deeply about his material craft throughout his career.

In 1905 Gilman and his new family paid a long visit to his wife's parents in Chicago, where his father-in-law, disapproving of the artist's profession, failed to persuade him to join the family business. A second daughter, Hannah, was born there and a year later, in London, a son, Richard, who died barely a year old. This tragedy may have exacerbated the couple's developing marital problems.

In February 1907 Gilman met Walter Sickert by chance and was immediately projected into his circle, where he found, among others, Spencer Gore, a fellow Slade student. The event was momentous for Gilman, and shaped his entire career. While he lived in various locations, mainly outside London, and with family ties, his art had developed quietly and without the progressive influences which were now to surround him. Gore and other Slade contemporaries and fellow travellers had become aware of Post-Impressionism and recent developments in French painting, including the work of Cézanne, Van Gogh and Gauguin. These young English artists struggling to be seen and heard in the exhibition halls of the native backward-looking and rejectionist art establishment urgently needed a leader and a banner to rally around. Sickert, already an established artist and a polemicist with a reputation as a non-conformist, was their man. His first choice of career as an actor having failed, after passing fleetingly through the Slade Sickert had worked as an assistant to James Macneill Whistler, with whom he travelled to the Continent. In Paris he met Edgar Degas, who became a lifelong friend and a seminal influence. In England, though a member of the NEAC, he was denigrated for his bawdy music-hall paintings by critics and the establishment, and found himself isolated when Steer abandoned Impressionism and Whistler made known his hostility. A further blow was the breakdown of his first marriage. In 1898 a demoralized Sickert had withdrawn to Dieppe, where he had spent part of his childhood, to lie low and paint the local architecture.

There, in 1905, while on a painting holiday in France, Spencer Gore was introduced to Sickert and both felt instant rapport. Sickert's reputation was well known to Gore, whose account of the talented new generation of artists awaiting guidance persuaded Sickert to return to London later that same year, initially for a

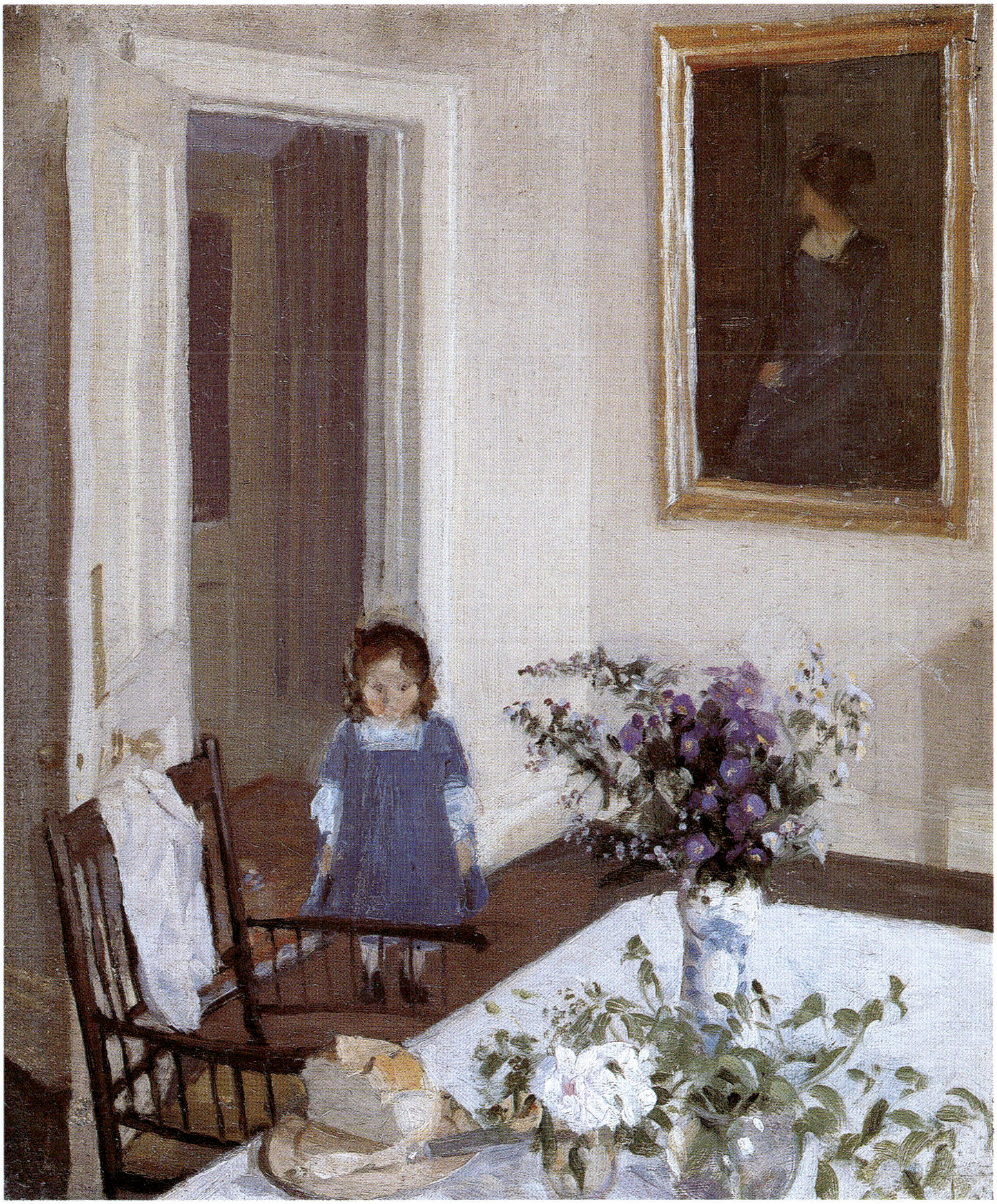

HAROLD GILMAN

Interior, *ca.* 1907–08

Oil on canvas, 350 × 360 mm

Southampton City Art Gallery

short stay. He was also drawn to London, perhaps, by his new-found interest in figure painting, of nude or partially clothed models inhabiting dark and sleazy bedrooms. Sickert knew the perfect place for such subject-matter, and accordingly installed himself in Camden Town, a once fashionable Regency area which had deteriorated into tenements and boarding houses after the building of nearby Euston, King's Cross and St Pancras stations. Sickert soon embarked on the custom of being 'at home' on Saturday afternoons in his Fitzroy Street studio to a growing number of sympathetic artists, and in the spring of 1907 decided to formalize this arrangement.

His plan was for the group to club together to purchase easels, to rent rooms close by, and to meet there regularly to promote and sell their art to invited patrons. In letters to the artists Ethel Sands and Nan Hudson he explained his idea:

"I do it for two reasons. Because it is more interesting to people to see the work of 7 or 9 people than one and because I want to keep up an incessant proselytizing agency to accustom people to mine and other painter's work of a modern character. Every week we would put something different on the easels. It is agreeable sometimes to show something 'lucky' you have done at once to anyone it may interest. All the painters interested could keep work there and would have keys and could show anything by anyone at any time [....] I want to create a Salon d'Automne milieu in London and you could both help me very much [....]

"Accustom people weekly to see work in a different notation from the current English one. Make it clear that we all have work for sale at prices that people of moderate means could afford. (That a picture costs less than a supper at the Savoy). Make known the work of painters who already are producing ripe work, but who are still elbowed or kept out by timidity etc [....]

"Further I particularly believe that I am sent from heaven to finish all your educations! And by ricochet, to receive a certain amount of instruction from the younger generation."[4]

Harold Gilman became a founder member of Sickert's Fitzroy Street Group, and slowly, but not immediately, the exposure to new ideas, new ways of seeing and making paintings and persistent discussion would begin to change his art practice. On the move again, in 1907 the Gilman family went to stay at Sickert's house in Neuville near Dieppe for the best part of a year, but then the idea of Letchworth must have begun to attract Gilman, whose socialist convictions matched the ethos of the new garden city. The following summer the Gilmans were in residence at no. 15, Westholm Green. Letchworth must have fulfilled their aspirations, for they commissioned Barry Parker to build a new and substantial

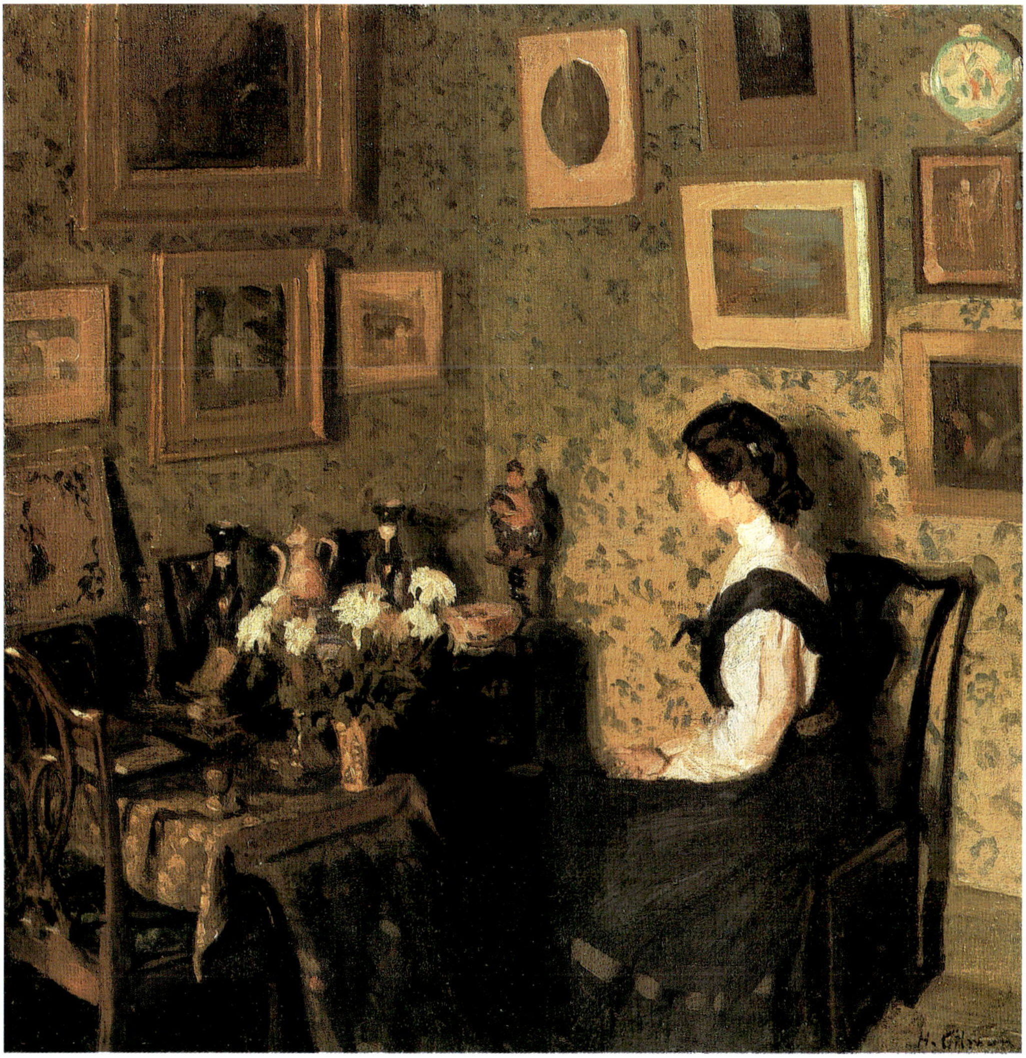

HAROLD GILMAN
Edwardian Interior, ca. 1907
Oil on canvas, 533 × 540 mm
Tate, London

house for the family. Gilman's grandfather Ellis had founded a tea company in Hong Kong and, although the family fortune diminished after his death, Harold's share of £400 was sufficient for the new house.[5] No. 100, Wilbury Road was to incorporate a north-lit studio at the back with a bedroom above, connected by a trapdoor so that Gilman could work undisturbed late into the night! In September a second son, David, was born but his parents' relationship was disintegrating, and when Grace took the children to Chicago the following summer it was for good. Gilman was devastated: always a devoted father, he missed them constantly and did his best to keep in touch.[6]

In Letchworth Gilman and Ratcliffe established an enduring and significant friendship. Gilman was taken with Ratcliffe's drawings of London buildings and encouraged him to take up oil painting. His powers of persuasion must have proved irresistible, for at the age of forty Ratcliffe abandoned his profession, graphic design, and became a full-time artist, which boded a precarious future. In 1910 Ratcliffe followed Gilman back to London and studied at the Slade for one term, part-time. Of more consequence, Gilman introduced Ratcliffe to the Fitzroy Group, and his art began to develop rapidly. A new and central influence was Lucien Pissarro. As a fountain of knowledge and living link to the great French modern movement, he made a substantial impression on the junior members of the group, including Gilman and Ratcliffe. It was Pissarro who advocated the technique of broken brushwork in pure and high-keyed colour.

By 1910 Sickert's original group, which was always dynamic, had already changed its personnel. Talented new members had been recruited through the Allied Artists Association, which had staged a dramatic inaugural exhibition in 1908 at the Albert Hall. Foreign artists had become fed up with investing trouble and expense in submitting work to the NEAC and other jury shows at which they were likely only to be rejected; the same problem faced many other English artists besides the Fitzroy Street Group. After considerable consultation and canvassing, Frank Rutter, art critic of *The Sunday Times*, established the jury-free AAA, modelled on the Parisian Salon des Indépendants. The organizers were swamped with subscriptions and with entries, many of which were of questionable quality. But Rutter persuaded the young artist and critic Walter Bayes to partake with the quip, "Why pay a shilling to see 2 thousand works at the academy when for the same money you can see 4 thousand at our exhibition?" It would, he boasted, be "bigger and worse than the Royal Academy!".[7] Bayes, together with Robert Bevan and Charles Ginner, both of whom had been practising forms of Post-Impressionism abroad, were discovered at the AAA exhibition by Sickert and his colleagues, and all three would join the Fitzroy Street Group.

In 1910 the influential art historian and artist Roger Fry organized the first of two exhibitions, for which he coined the term 'Post-Impressionism', that both had a major impact and far-reaching consequences on the Fitzroy Street Group. Work by Gauguin, Van Gogh, Cézanne, Matisse, Picasso and others was on public display in strength for the first time in London. Predictably the art establishment, including the NEAC, the critics and the

opposite
WILLIAM RATCLIFFE
In the Sun, *ca.* 1911
Oil on canvas, 457 x 356 mm
Courtesy of the National Museums and Galleries on Merseyside, Walker Art Gallery

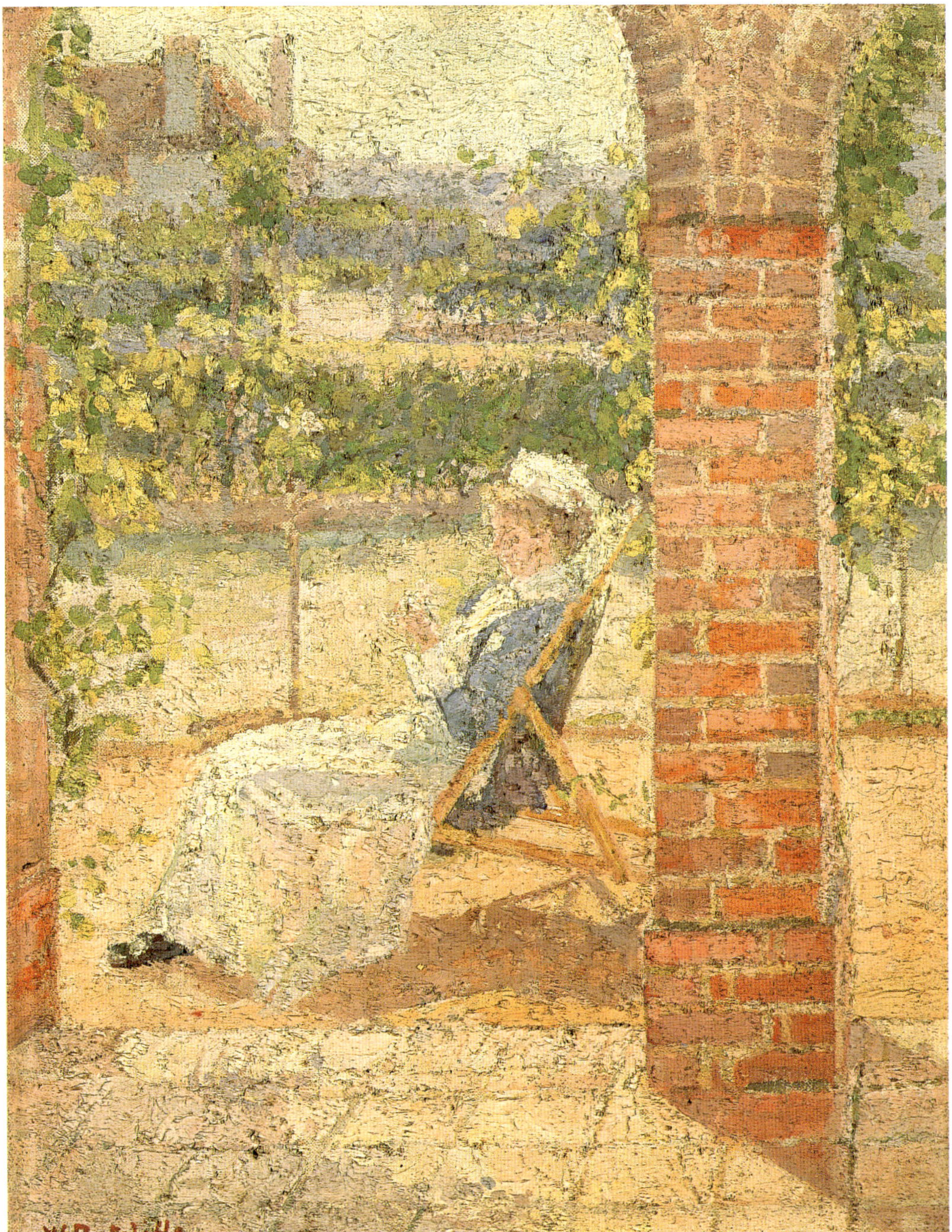
W. Ratcliffe.

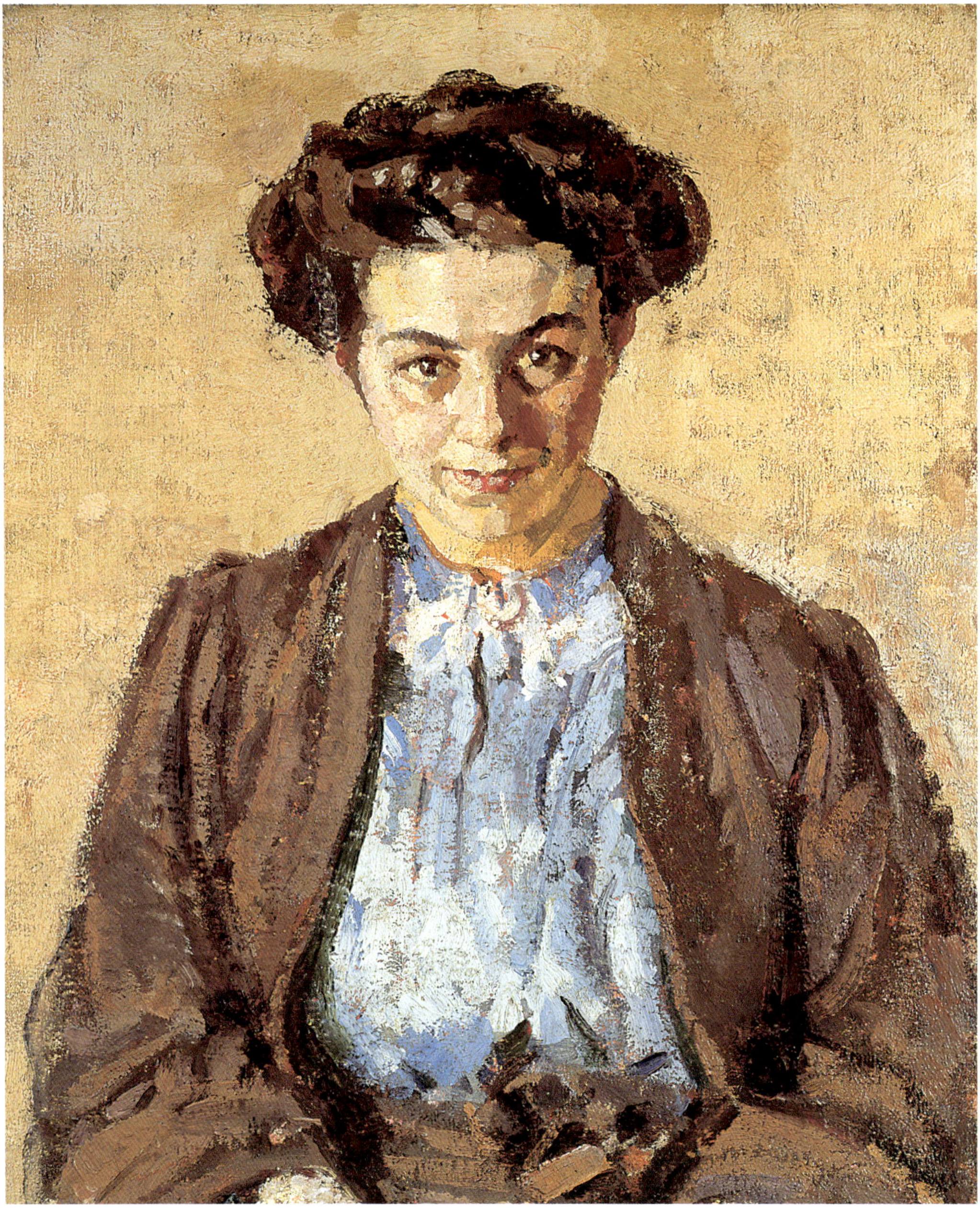

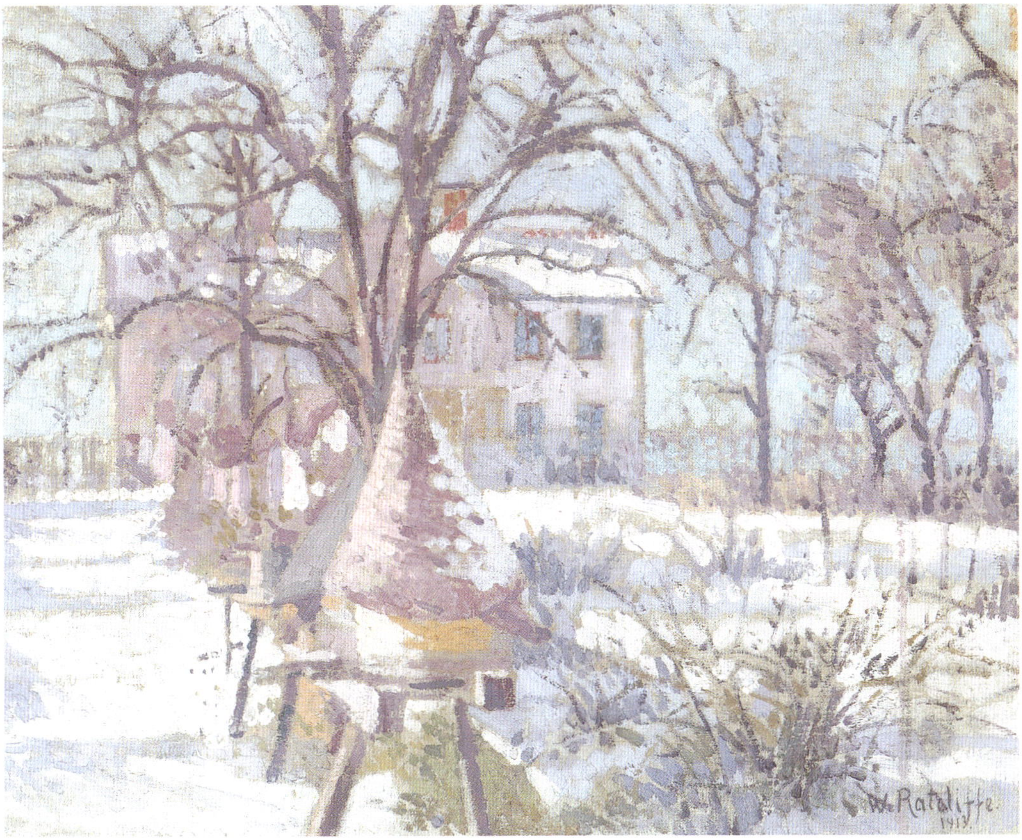

above
WILLIAM RATCLIFFE
Beehives in the Snow, Sweden, 1913
Oil on canvas, 425 x 510 mm
Government Art Collection UK

left
HAROLD GILMAN
The Blue Blouse
(Elèni Zompolides), *ca.* 1910
Oil on canvas, 609 x 457 mm
Leeds City Art Gallery

public were outraged by the pictures, but the exhibition only served to strengthen the resolve of the Fitzroy Street Group and accelerate their stylistic development. It must have been a heady and exciting time. The group interchanged ideas, subject-matter and experimental painting techniques. Gilman slowly loosened his brushwork, using brighter local colour in a more contemporary and Post-Impressionist idiom. Sound draughtsmanship and subtle tonal relationships remained, but Gilman now applied his paint with a new bravura – raw and direct in impastoed blobs and smears. In 1910, following Sickert and Gore, though from a more confrontational perspective than theirs, Gilman became interested in painting nudes – a radical departure from his earlier work – and occasionally, influenced by Ginner, urban landscape. Ratcliffe's technique at this time followed chiefly Pissarro's example, consisting of small, dry, stippled touches of paint compacted together. The two artists sometimes shared subject-matter. Their paintings of Clarence Gardens near Fitzroy Street emphasize their different approaches, for while Ratcliffe was interested in recording incidental detail Gilman concentrated on formal structure.

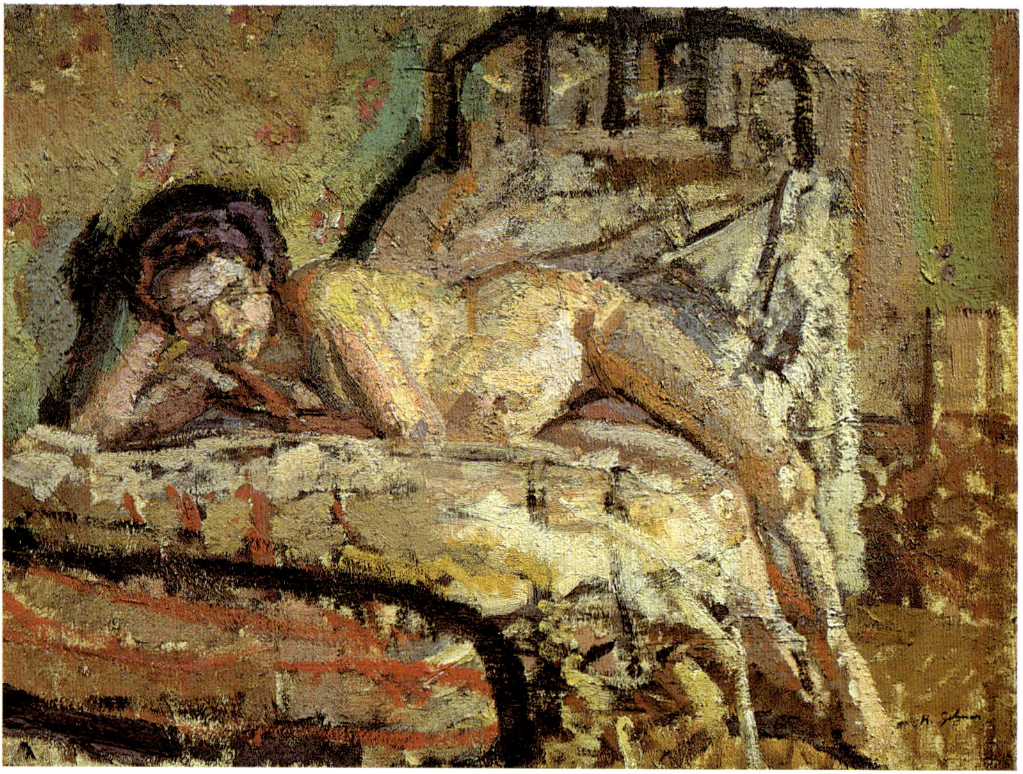

HAROLD GILMAN
The Model (Reclining Nude),
ca. 1911
Oil on canvas, 457 x 610 mm
Arts Council Collection, Hayward Gallery, London
Photography by John Webb

The various influences of different Post-Impressionist masters may have been confusing initially for Gilman, but after a propitious visit to Paris in late 1910 with Ginner and Rutter to see various collections of modern paintings, he eventually declared, like Ginner, for Van Gogh. He believed Van Gogh to be the master of Realism and a true humanitarian.

The hostility of the traditional London art world towards Fry's Post-Impressionist exhibition extinguished for ever any remaining hope for the Fitzroy Street Group of exhibiting at the NEAC. They were therefore led to found their own exhibiting platform, as the sixteen-member Camden Town Group. After heated discussion the artists included were, wrote Ginner, "considered to be the best and most promising of the day".[8] Gilman successfully proposed Ratcliffe. He and Sickert were adamant that women were to be excluded, since many of their acquaintance were amateurs, which they felt would give the wrong impression.

The first two Camden Town Group exhibitions were held at the Carfax Gallery in June and December 1911, but proved both critically and financially only a moderate success. Several members decided upon new prospects and a change of scene in 1912. In the summer of that year Gilman lent his Letchworth house, which

HAROLD GILMAN
Nude on a Bed, 1911–12
Oil on canvas, 610 x 508 mm
York City Art Gallery

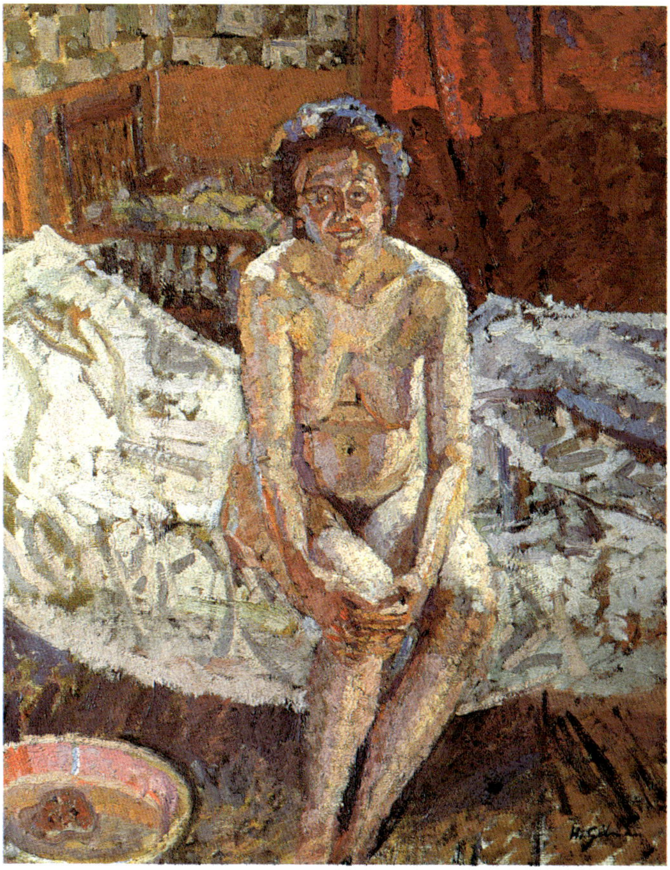

he had rarely occupied, to Spencer Gore, while he himself visited Sweden. Little is known of Gilman's visit or why he chose to go there. It might have been a welcome distraction for him after a failed attempt to visit his children in Chicago.[9] Artistically the trip was immensely productive and successful. Gilman painted a few interiors but engaged himself most seriously and energetically with the subject of landscape, inspired no doubt by the rugged wilderness lit by the clear northern light. Rendering it faithfully and conveying the subtleties of aerial perspective while applying his new-found Post-Impressionist principles presented him with particular difficulties. He was adventurous in his response, using thick bands of impasto to project the sky forward, and flatter, abstract areas of colour, or alternatively Van Gogh-like brushwork, to represent the forms.[10] His choice of subject-matter was less so, however. Whereas Gore, stimulated by the new world of Letchworth, was painting modern subjects such as the railway station, the more conservative Gilman avoided the contemporary and focused upon traditional, picturesque motifs – bridges and harvest scenes in homage to Van Gogh.

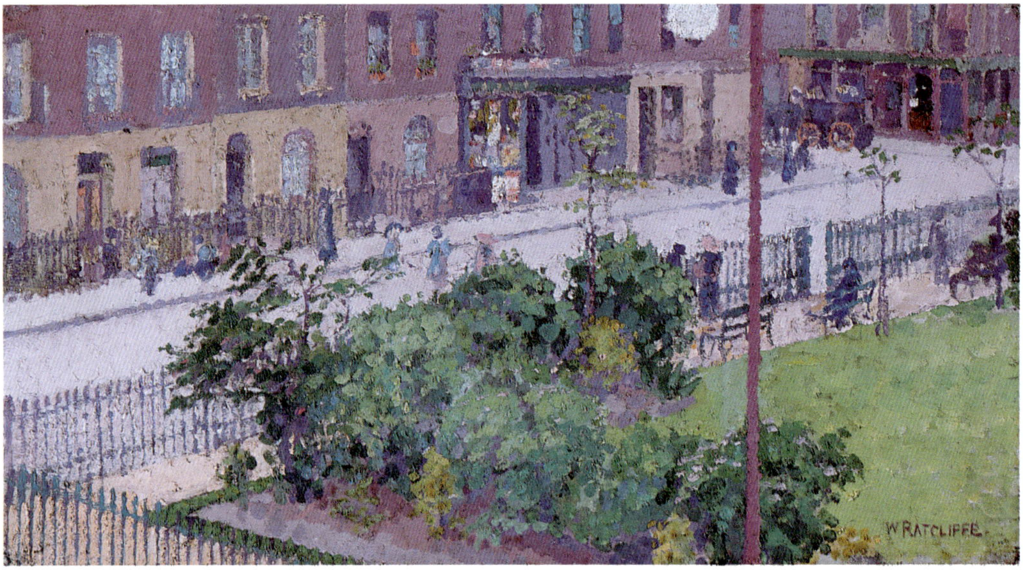
W RATCLIFFE

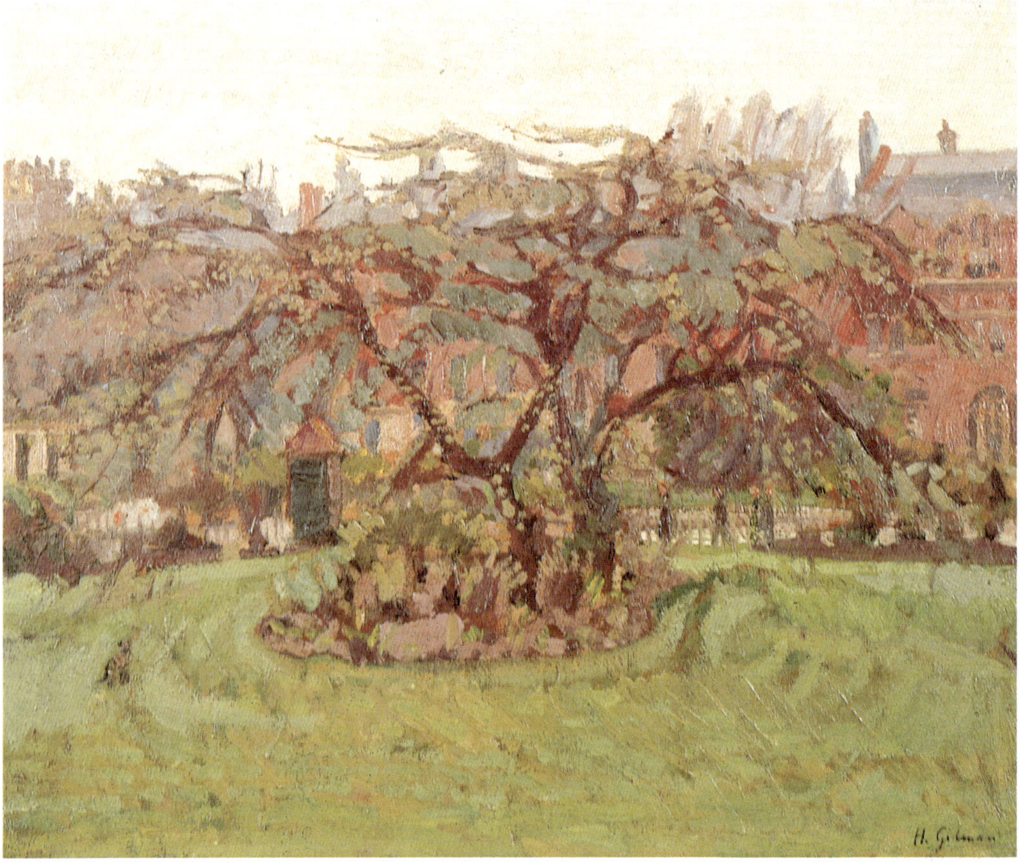
H. Gilman

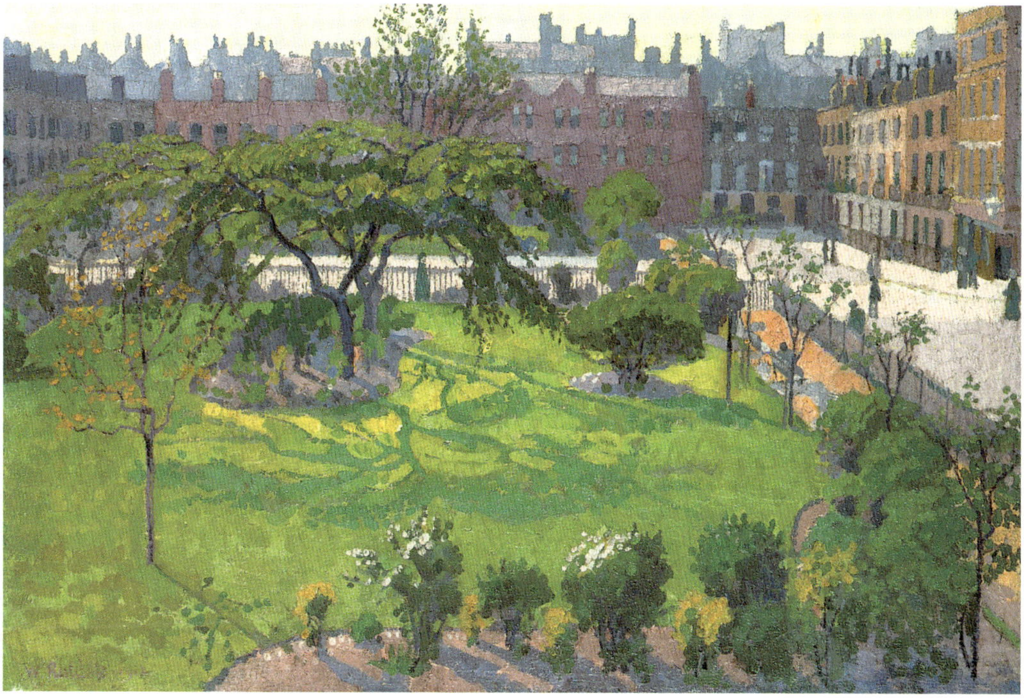

above
WILLIAM RATCLIFFE
Clarence Gardens, 1912
Oil on canvas, 508 x 762 mm
Tate, London
© 2002 the artist's estate

left above
WILLIAM RATCLIFFE
Clarence Gardens, 1912
Oil on canvas, 340 x 572 mm
Private collection
© 2002 the artist's estate

left below
HAROLD GILMAN
Clarence Gardens NW, *ca.* 1912
Oil on canvas, 508 x 61 mm
Ferens Art Gallery, Hull

Ratcliffe had exhibited in public for the first time at the inaugural Camden Town Group exhibition; his work was amongst the cheapest there! Subsequently he must have been impressed with Gilman's account of his Scandinavian trip and with what he had painted there, for he decided to follow suit. Fortuitously Stanley Parker's Swedish wife had recently assisted her brother to purchase an estate at Sundsholm, Färholt, in Kalmar in south-eastern Sweden;[11] together with the connoisseur J.W. Beresford, Ratcliffe and the Parkers set out for a protracted visit there early in 1913. It is possible that Gilman accompanied them for part of the journey, while on his way to Norway. While based at Sundsholm, Ratcliffe was invigorated by creative inspiration in much the same way as his mentor had been and entered a phase of vigorous productivity – which would be very much the high point of his artistic career. Ratcliffe's aptitude for constructing dense and complex patterns combined with an experimental response to perspective to produce some vivid paintings. The sharp northern light heightened his colour values, which became dominated by deep pinks, purples and blue greens. His paint handling remained impastoed, controlled and tight, but the stippled brushwork gave way to a flatter mosaic of dazzling, abstract shapes. This new-found confidence was also reflected in larger-scale canvases. Ratcliffe remained in Sweden possibly until early summer.

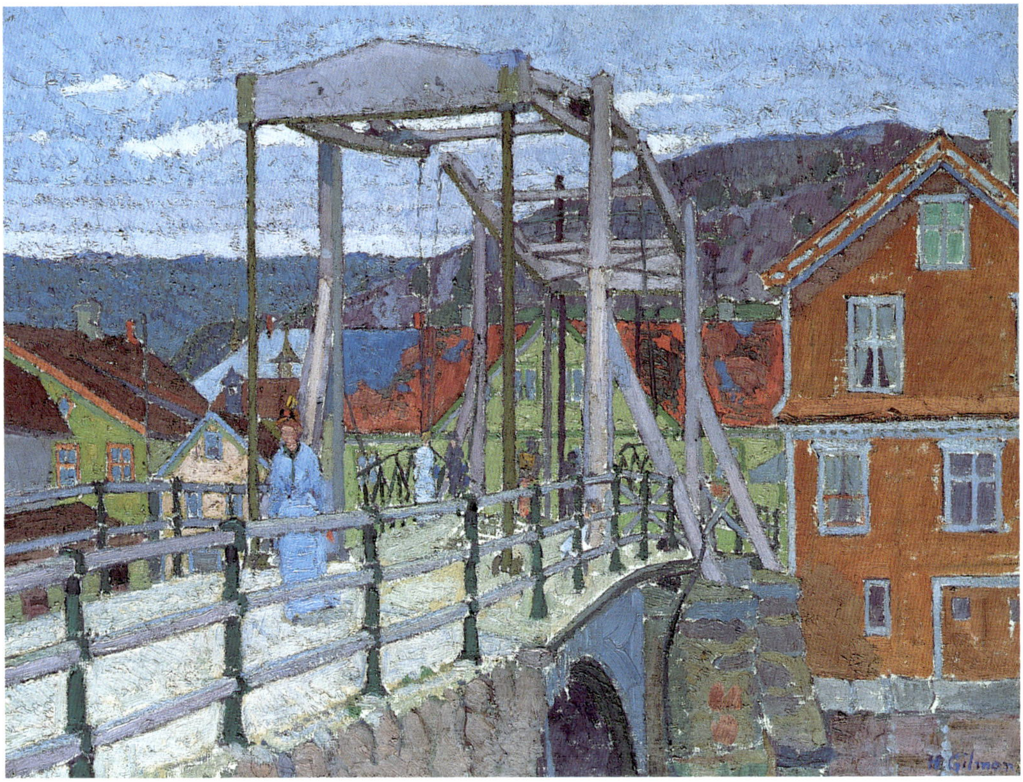

HAROLD GILMAN
Canal Bridge, Flekkefjord,
ca. 1913–14
Oil on canvas, 457 x 610 mm
Tate, London

Gilman, meanwhile, was making further progress with his painting in Norway during the summer. He was still experimenting with style but his landscapes of bridges and mountains express more resolve and confidence than he had shown earlier. His work there is often evocative of Courbet, with broad and direct brushwork in dark blues, greens and purples.

Gilman's career from 1914 to his death in 1919

By 1912 the enthusiasm, conviction and supportive ethos of the fledgling Camden Town Group was failing. Avant-garde art politics were descending rapidly into turmoil. The group staged what would be its final exhibition in December 1912, just two months after Roger Fry's second Post-Impressionist exhibition at the Grafton Gallery, which this time included British artists. Now the critics and public could see that the Camden Town Group did not constitute a coherent movement but was a disparate band of artists with different philosophies who coincidentally exhibited together. Of the sixteen members Augustus John, James Innes, Henry Lamb, Walter Bayes and Duncan Grant (a replacement for

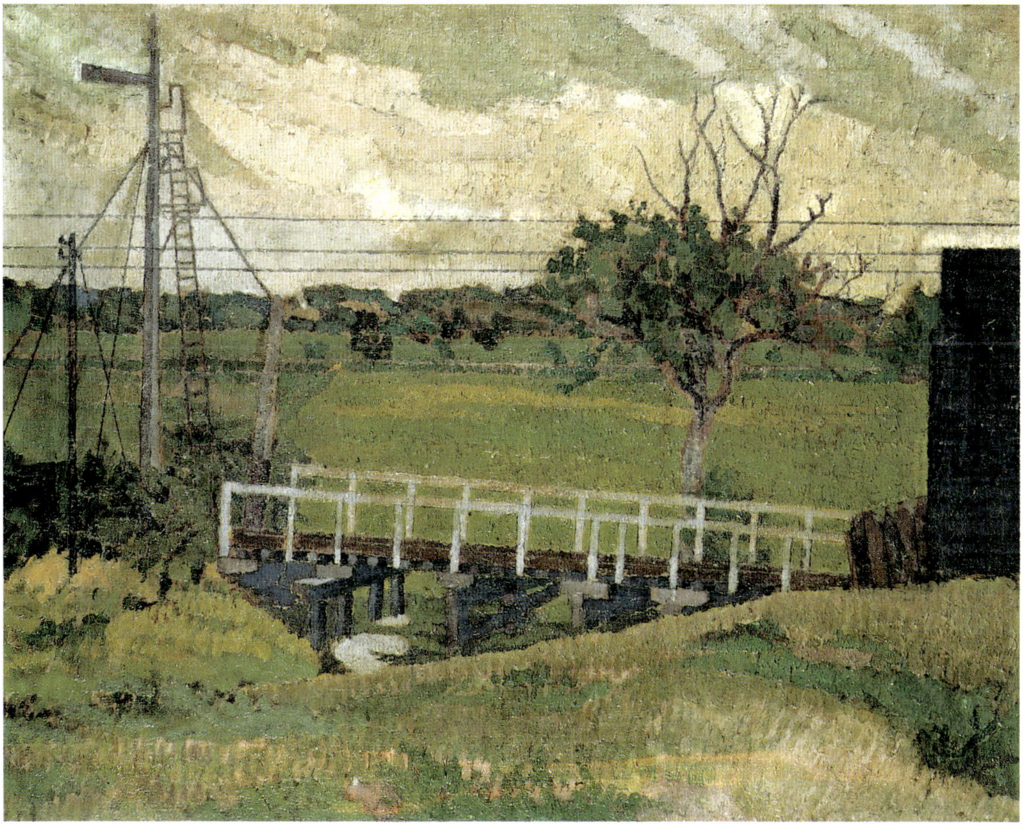

WILLIAM RATCLIFFE
Bridge, Sweden, ca. 1913
Oil on canvas, 408 x 510 mm
Private collection

Maxwell Lightfoot, who took his own life in 1911) were not regulars at Fitzroy Street, which was reflected in their work. John and Innes were romantics more at home in North Wales or the South of France than recording the everyday scene in urban London. Lamb and Grant, whose only contribution was one painting at the second exhibition, were rooted more firmly in the rival avant-garde camp of Roger Fry and Vanessa Bells's Grafton Group. However, Percy Wyndham Lewis, a Slade student, who had travelled to Madrid with Spencer Gore in 1902, was the main catalyst for the break-up. Gore and Gilman had persuaded Sickert that Lewis should be included from the outset, but by 1911 he was developing his own brand of Cubism, painting turbulent vortices of distorted form which soon became known as Vorticism. This work stood out as entirely at odds with that of the more homogeneous Fitzroy Street artists, with their objective realism of urban life translated by means of "a clean and solid mosaic of thick paint in a light key."[12] Lewis had a reputation as an argumentative and volatile character and upset many, not least Sickert, to whom his output was anathema.

In December 1913 the Camden Town Group was officially

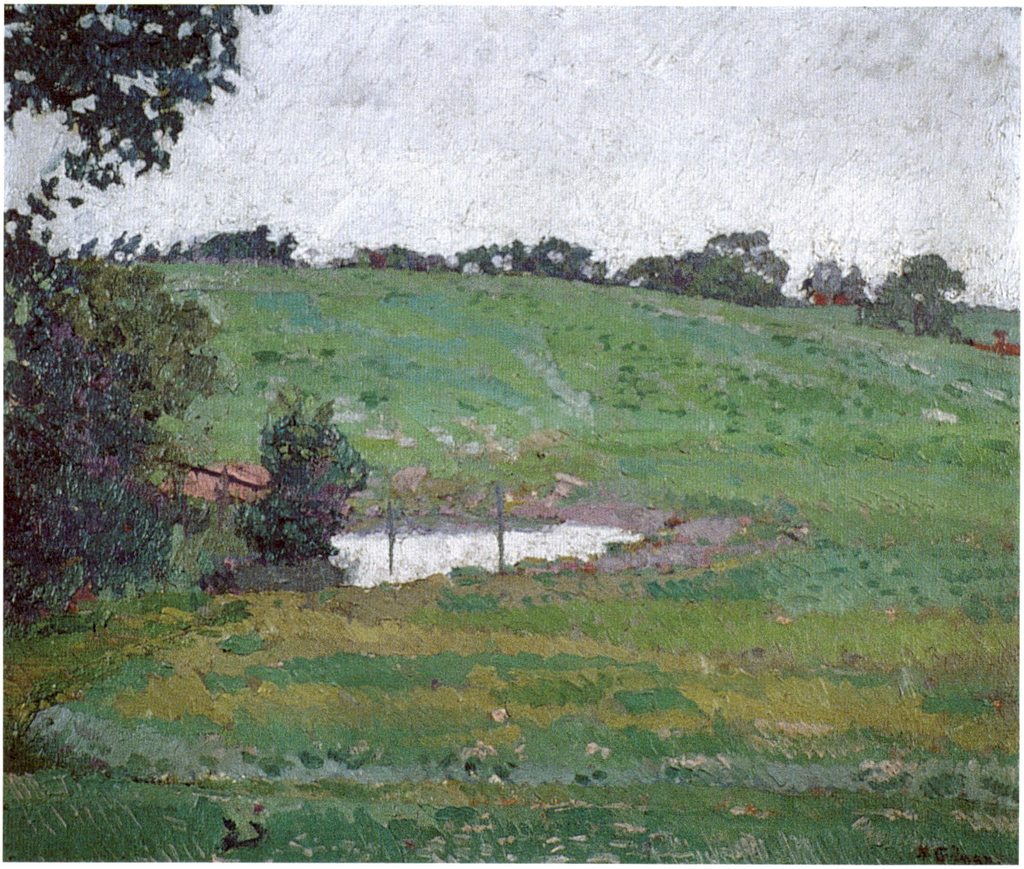

HAROLD GILMAN
Norwegian Landscape, 1913
Oil on canvas, 510 x 610 mm
Government Art Collection UK

invited to present an exhibition at Brighton entitled *English Post-Impressionists, Cubists and Others*. The Vorticists, including Lewis, David Bomberg, Christopher Nevinson, Jacob Epstein, Frederick Etchells, Cuthbert Hamilton and Edward Wadsworth, were separated physically and in the catalogue from the Fitzroy Street artists. There were further divisions behind the scenes. In a letter to Nan Hudson Sickert wrote, "I am afraid you will think me more swing of the Pendulum than ever. But like the lady in bridal attire who bolts at the church door the Epstein-Lewis marriage is too much for me and I have bolted. I have resigned both Fitzroy Street and the London Group [....] First Gilman forced Epstein on me, as you know against my will. But I was in a minority. At Brighton the Epstein-Lewis-Etchells room made me sick and I publicly disengaged my responsibility [....] I don't believe in them, and further, I think they render any consideration of serious painting impossible."[13] Lucien Pissarro followed suit. It was clear that the Camden Town Group had run its course and was now outmoded. Ironically, Sickert, whose visionary efforts to champion the lot of

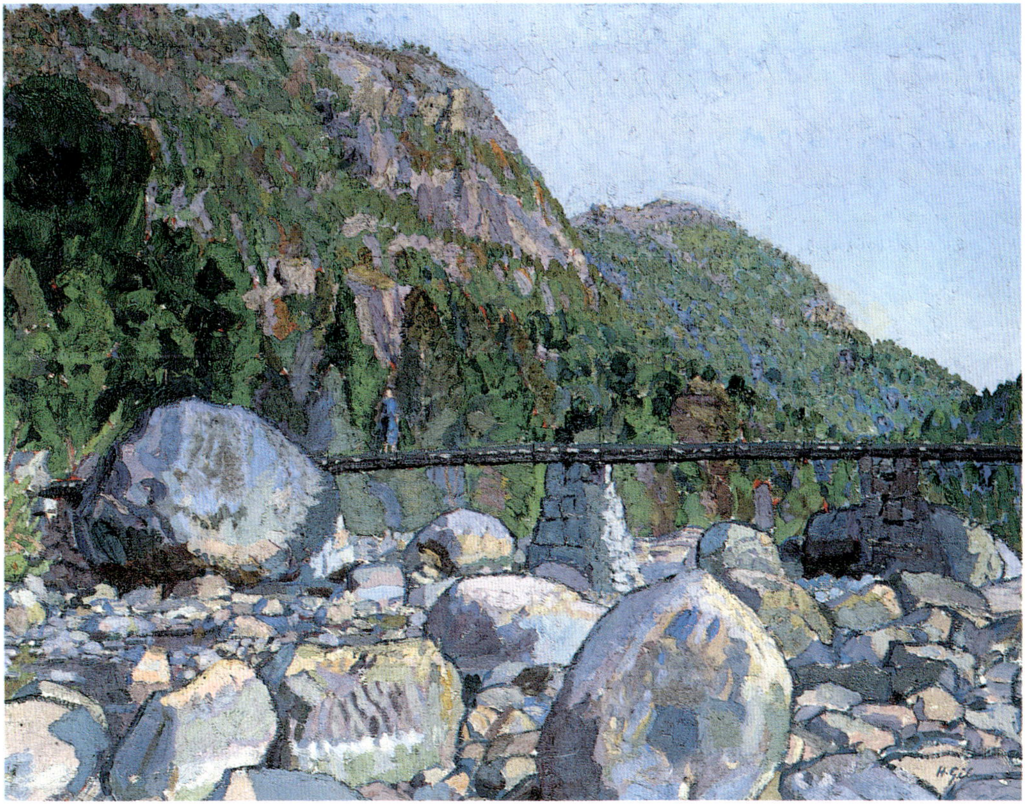

HAROLD GILMAN
The Mountain Bridge, Norway, 1913
Oil on canvas, 620 x 800 mm
Worthing Museum and Art Gallery
Photography by Mike Fear

the young, progressive English artists had succeeded beyond his expectations, was now himself overtaken by modernism. However, the different avant-garde factions that had recently emerged soon felt the need to consolidate. Thus the London Group (which still survives today) rose phoenix-like from the ashes of the Camden Town Group; its first meeting took place on 25 October 1913. Gilman was made president and this time women were allowed membership.

After 1911 Sickert's influence on Gilman had diminished, as he grew closer to Charles Ginner and to the inspiration of Van Gogh and the use of pure colour. Wyndham Lewis humorously recorded Gilman's conversion from Sickert's dark palettes: "He would look over in the direction of Sickert's studio and a slight shudder would convulse him as he thought of the little brown worm of paint that was possibly, even at that moment, struggling out on to the palette that held no golden chromes, emerald green, vermilions, only, as it, of course, should do."[14]

Although the Camden Town Group had effectively expanded to become the London Group, its original members formed still smaller splinter groups. Gilman joined with Ginner, Bevan and

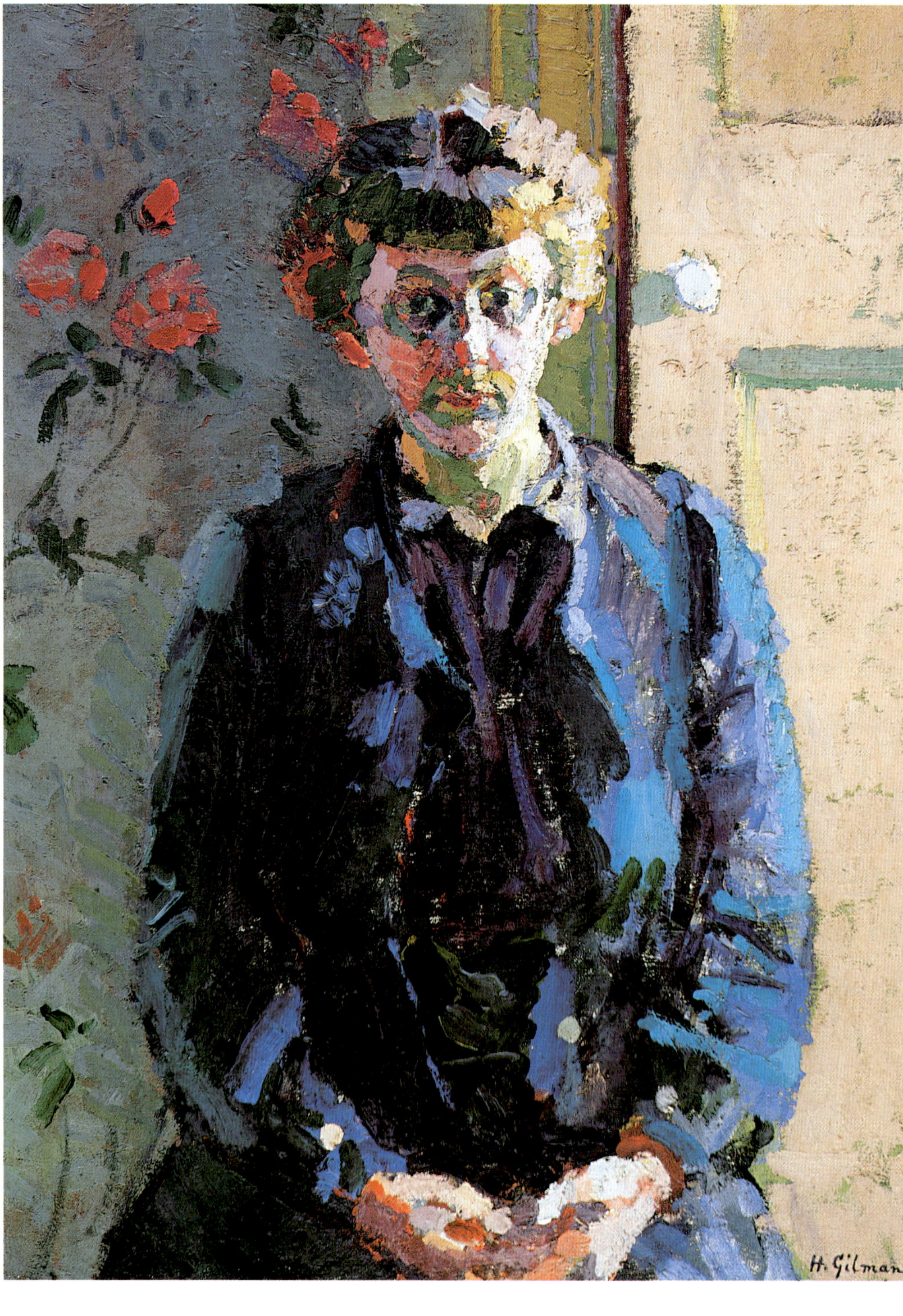
H. Gilman

HAROLD GILMAN
Sylvia Gosse, 1913
Oil on canvas, 695 x 513 mm
Southampton City Art Gallery

others to form the Cumberland Market Group, named this time after the address of Bevan's studio. Here the new group continued to conduct 'at homes' on Saturdays in the same manner as at Fitzroy Street (with plenty of strong tea and slab cake!). Gilman and Ginner were sufficiently close artistically to exhibit together at the Goupil Gallery in April 1914 and to issue their own manifesto – a fashionable activity for avant-garde factions – entitled *Neo-Realism*. The chief thrust of their argument was that the artist should always return to nature and make his own interpretation from it first-hand. Ginner rejected "naturalism" as "the production of a Realist with a poor mind", who would copy nature "with a dull and common eye" but with "no personal vision, no individual temperament".[15] They denigrated artists who adopted formulae or made pastiches from the individual styles of the great Post-Impressionists, Van Gogh, Gauguin and Cézanne. In an article in the magazine *New Age* in January 1914, Ginner wrote: "The Academic painters merely adopt the visions which the creative artists drew from the source of nature itself. They adopt the mannerisms, which is all they are capable of seeing in the work of the creative artist, and make formulas out of them. They are copyists. They are poor of mind."[16] Both Ginner and Gilman were perfectionists regarding the handling of paint. They rejected "slapdash, careless and slick painting". The true Neo-Realist, according to Ginner, practised "good and sound craftsmanship [….] Furthermore, in this matter of medium, it is only out of a sound and solid pigment that good surface and variety can be got, and durability in ages to come."[17]

Such assertive and suggestive statements stirred Sickert into public action. In a series of savage spats conducted in *The New Age* Sickert began by agreeing that "Art that is based on other art tends to become atrophied", but then argued vehemently against the use of impastoed paint for its own sake. Sickert's mentor, Degas, had advocated a smooth surface. When Gilman replied in a letter entitled *The Worst Critic in London*, Sickert swiftly countered with another piece headed *The Thickest Painters in London!*.[18] Finally an enraged Ginner retorted that "he would paint as thick as he damn well pleased!".[19]

During 1914 Gilman moved to a new and more permanent address in London, at no. 47, Maple Street. His landlady was the redoubtable Mrs Mounter, whom Gilman was to celebrate and dignify in a series of outstanding portraits. At this time he was considering solutions to a technical problem. His progressive developments in Scandinavia had liberated him from the constraints of his early tonal training. But the use of pure and brilliant colour to describe natural and man-made form in terms of a complex pattern of interlocking planes was tending towards a merging of shapes. Following the example of Gore and Bevan, he solved the problem by employing dark outlines together with flatter, more defined areas of colour, a device he had previously rejected – indeed he had entitled a painting exhibited at the Allied Artists Association in 1912 *Thou Shalt Not Put a Blue Line Round Thy Mother!*[20] His work became ever more analytical and distilled, evoking a sense of ascetic quiescence. Pictorial composition and its detail was consistently and carefully considered with uncompromising precision. Gilman always needed to respond directly from nature, and though he experimented with forms of Cubism and other progressive conventions they held no lasting interest. His subject-matter remained conservative and traditionally middle-class. In the last years of his life he returned to explore the same subjects that had occupied his early years – domestic interiors and their inhabitants. He loved to paint everyday objects, teapots or chairs, whatever was to hand – the familiar and friendly. Spencer Gore once referred affectionately to one of his still lifes as "Gilman's breakfast",[21] and his friend Hubert Wellington described him as a "very English *Intimiste*".[22] His sublime late interiors, many painted at Maple Street with its trademark wallpaper design, represent the culmination of his career – a distinct and emphatically English development of Post-Impressionism.

In March 1914, tragically, Spencer Gore died after contracting pneumonia while painting at Richmond Park in the rain. This was a significant blow to any remaining coherence amongst the original Fitzroy Street Group, since Gore, the president of the Camden Town Group, had acted as peacemaker. The collaborative and supportive environment which was so essential to the development of the style and character of the Group's painting was finally extinguished. However, the *coup de grâce* was dealt to the hopes and fortunes of Gilman and his colleagues after the previous years of formative achievement by the onset of world war. Since he was unable to serve in the forces owing to his hip disability, though his two brothers fought in the trenches, the war seemed, in some respects, to pass Gilman by. His old injury perhaps contributed to his uncertain temper and obstinacy, for, though he rarely complained, he believed in the main that his life was difficult and that fate had dealt him a poor hand.

Gore had earlier 'inherited' Sickert's prime teaching post at Westminster School of Art and on his death Gilman took it over, only to have it confiscated by Sickert himself in 1915, much to his consternation. Subsequently he and Ginner started up their own art school evening classes at no. 16, Little Pulteney Street in Soho, but Gilman closed it down when Ginner was called up in 1917. Marjorie Lilly, one of the students, recalled that the regulars greatly

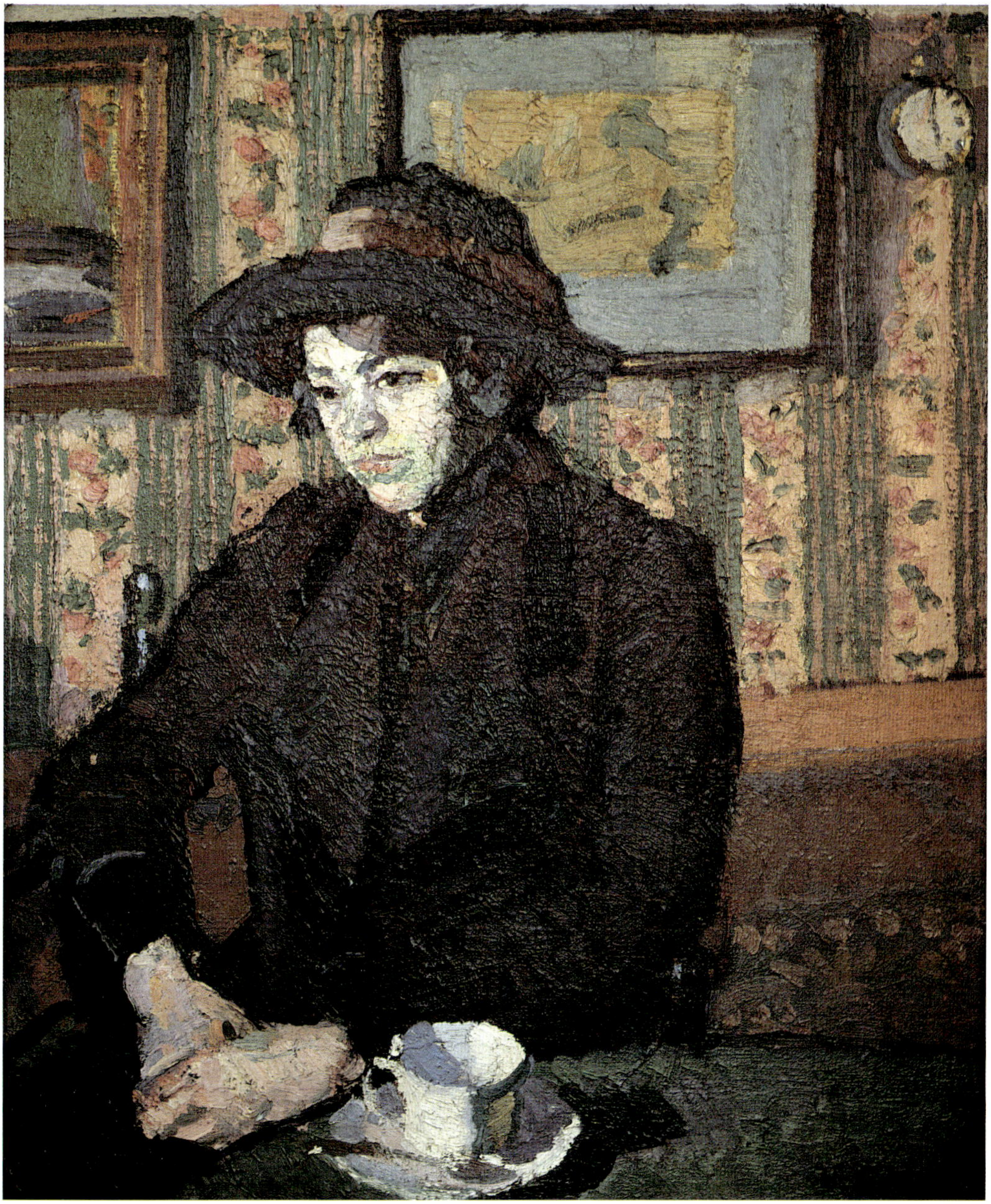

HAROLD GILMAN

Girl with a Teacup, ca. 1914

Oil on canvas, 622 × 521 mm

Private collection

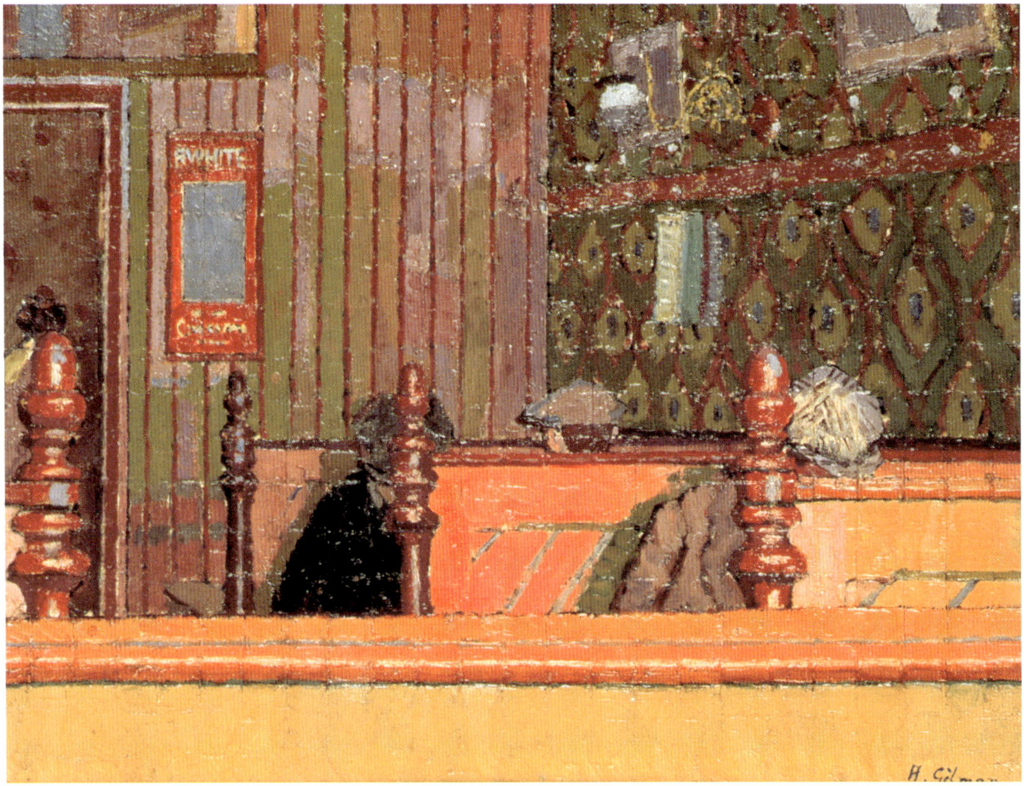

HAROLD GILMAN
An Eating House, 1913–14
Oil on canvas, 572 x 749 mm
Graves Art Gallery, Sheffield

enjoyed the sessions, until driven away by bombs. After his divorce came through in the same year Gilman married Sylvia Hardy, whom he had met when she was a student at the Westminster School a few years before. The couple moved to Hampstead and their son John was born in December.

Together with other British artists, including Ginner, Gilman was commissioned by the Canadian Government to produce a painting for their War Records Commission. Gilman was not enthusiastic and accepted the work merely because he was short of funds. His subject was the harbour at Halifax, Novia Scotia, where a merchant ship, loaded with ammunition, had exploded, killing several hundred people and destroying part of the town. In appalling weather Gilman made many sketches, from which he constructed a large painting on his return to England. Such was his disdain for the project that he chose to portray the damaged harbour from across the bay, thus reducing all the assembled machinery of war to a diminutive scale, dwarfed by the sea, sky and foreground.

Early in 1919, during the great European 'flu epidemic, hearing that Ginner had been struck down, Gilman went to him at once and nursed him, but contracted the disease himself. Both

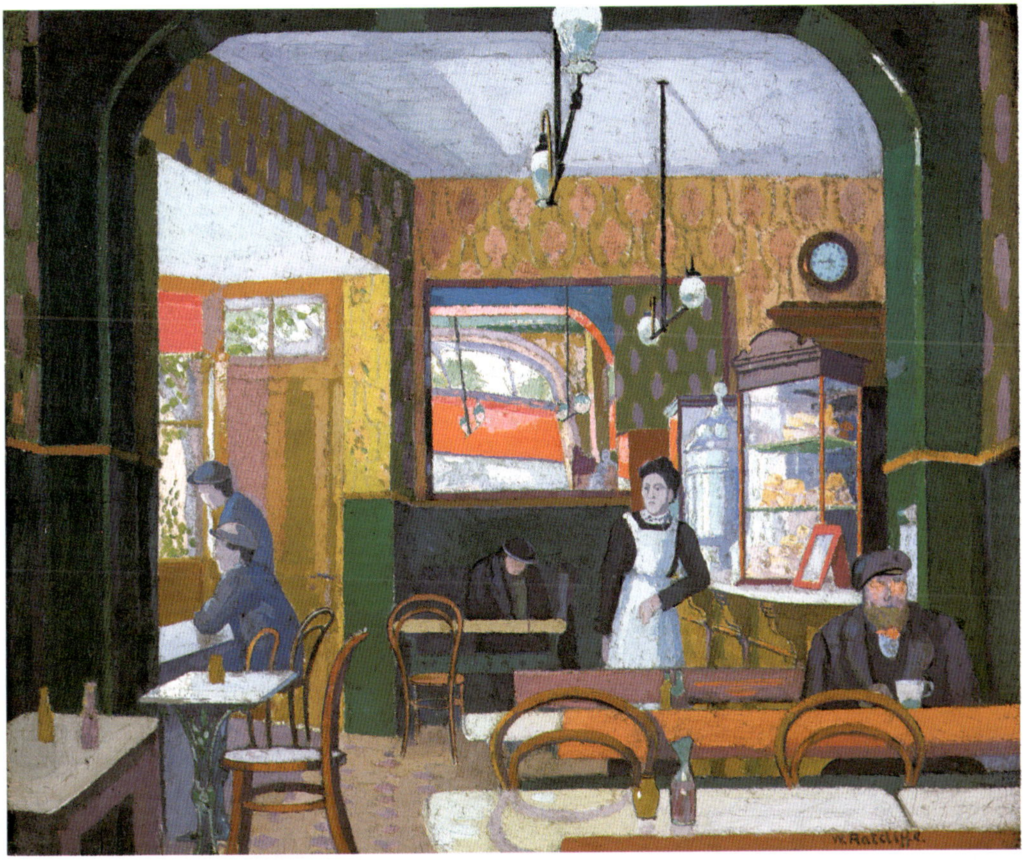

WILLIAM RATCLIFFE
The Coffee House, East Finchley, 1914
Oil on canvas, 510 × 613 mm
Southampton City Art Gallery

developed pneumonia, of which Gilman died. Ginner survived and worked avidly on alone until his own death in 1952. Gilman's death at the age of forty-three was a tragic loss, for there is no doubt his art would have developed further.

William Ratcliffe's career from 1914 to 1955

When William Ratcliffe moved to London he was unable to settle permanently but lived at various addresses, including Hampstead Garden Suburb, Belsize Park and Southill Park. He continued to paint the urban landscape, especially Hampstead and the river front, delighting in details such as railings, lamp-posts and other street furniture. After his Swedish visit his painting technique, incorporating a dry and dense application of paint built up in stippled touches, was replaced by broader, hard-edge brushwork with thinner paint and darker, stronger colour.

Together with this shift came an emphasis on formal pictorial design, as is evident in one of his most celebrated works, *The Coffee House, East Finchley*, 1914. The painting was influenced again

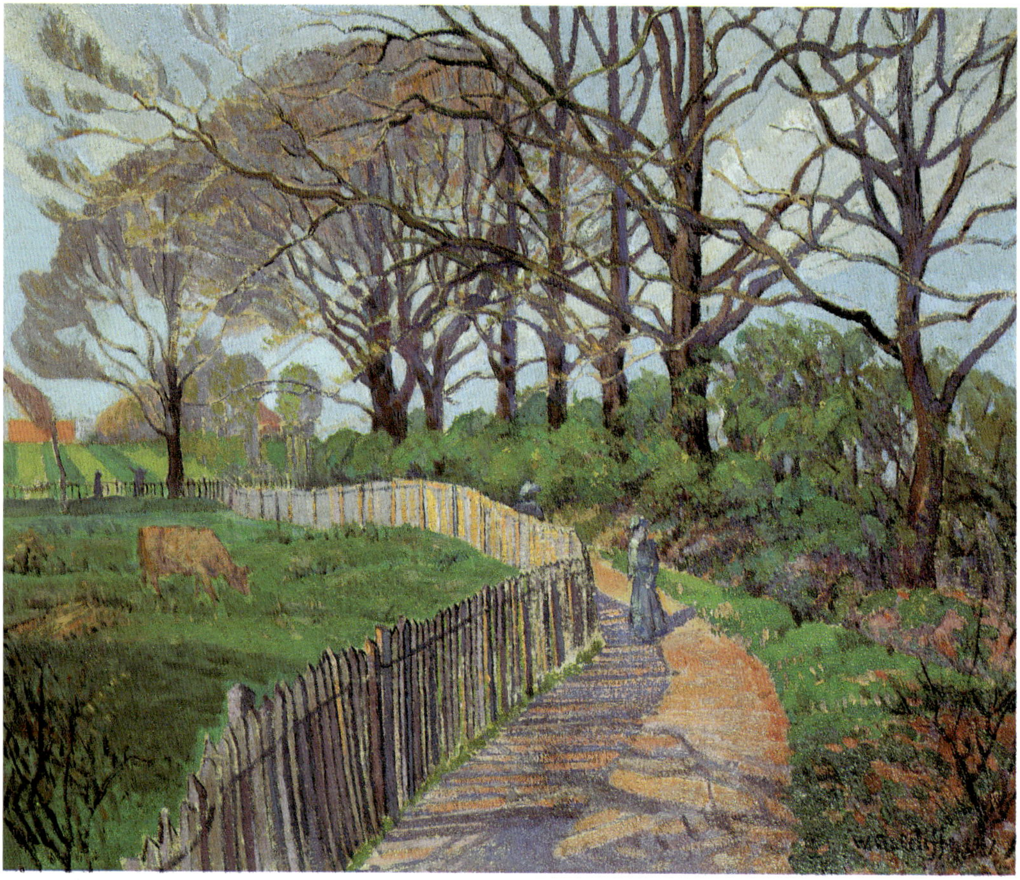

WILLIAM RATCLIFFE
Landscape with Cow, 1917
Oil on canvas, 508 × 610 mm
Leeds City Art Gallery

by Gilman, who had previously painted similar subjects, notably *An Eating House*, 1913–14. A letter Ratcliffe wrote to the Curator at Southampton City Art Gallery in 1953 describes how he came to make the painting:

"I well remember the time it was painted, just before the first war was started. I was then living in the Hampstead Garden Suburb and discovered this coffee house at East Finchley and went in to lunch one day and afterwards started a drawing sitting on the back seat with the sunlit red blind behind me and reflected in the mirror opposite. I was interested enough to carry on for several days and used to walk over the fields to Finchley almost daily until I had enough information for the picture which was progressing at home at the same time."[23]

Ratcliffe joined the London Group at its inception and exhibited there regularly until Gilman's death. After 1919 he gradually became disillusioned with the changing nature of the membership as more Vorticist and Bloomsbury artists joined, Roger Fry and his faction having gained effective control after 1917. Thereafter he

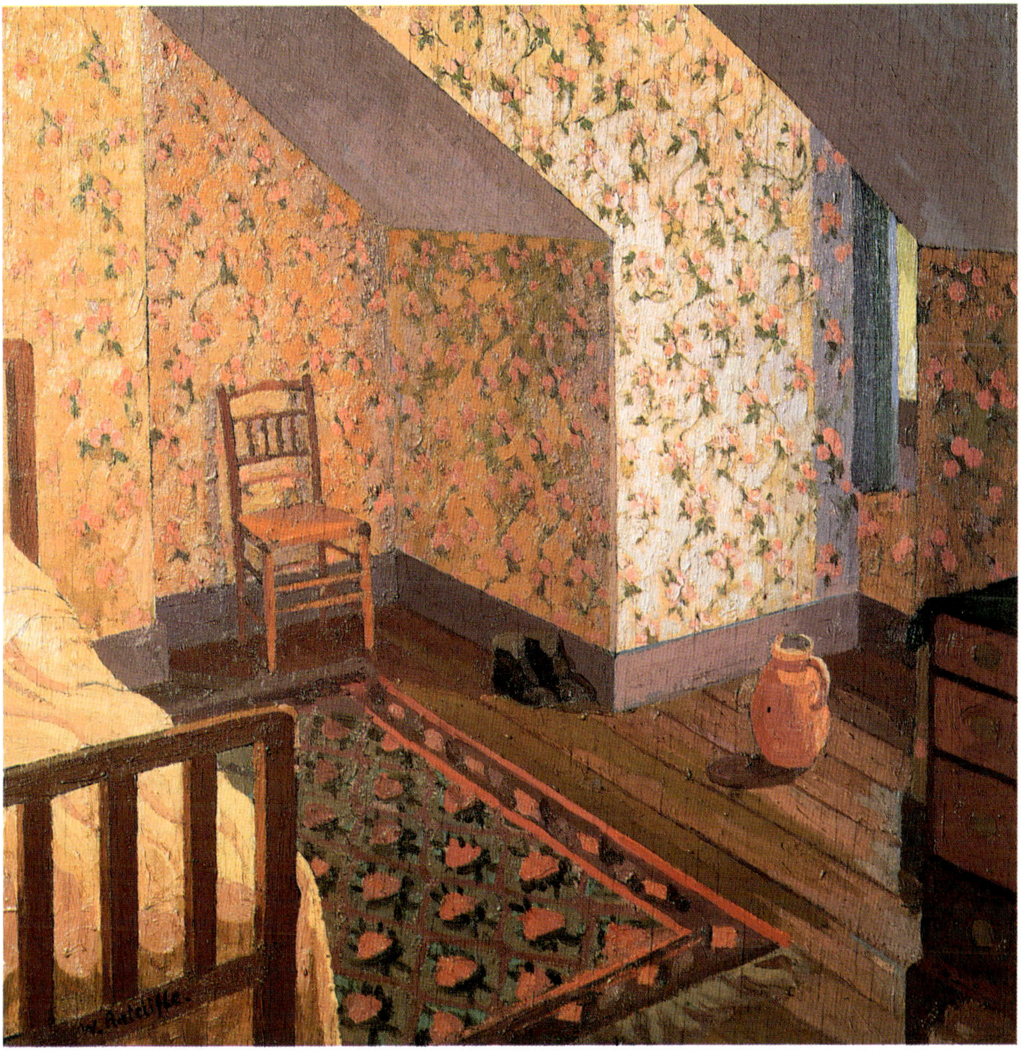

WILLIAM RATCLIFFE
The Attic Room, 1918
Oil on wood, 508 × 508 mm
Tate, London
Photography by John Webb

exhibited with the group only sporadically until 1926, and resigned in 1930.

Apart from his early formal training Ratcliffe owed his artistic development and outlook entirely to Gilman and the Fitzroy Street Group. Although, being inordinately shy, he did not contribute greatly to discussion, he would have absorbed much of the proceedings. Certainly his painting flourished in that environment. Like other less well-known members of the group such as Malcolm Drummond, he needed the stimulus of his more talented colleagues to produce fine work and when the group folded the impetus was lost. The death of his friend and mentor Gilman affected him deeply.

To some extent, after becoming an artist, Ratcliffe had led a

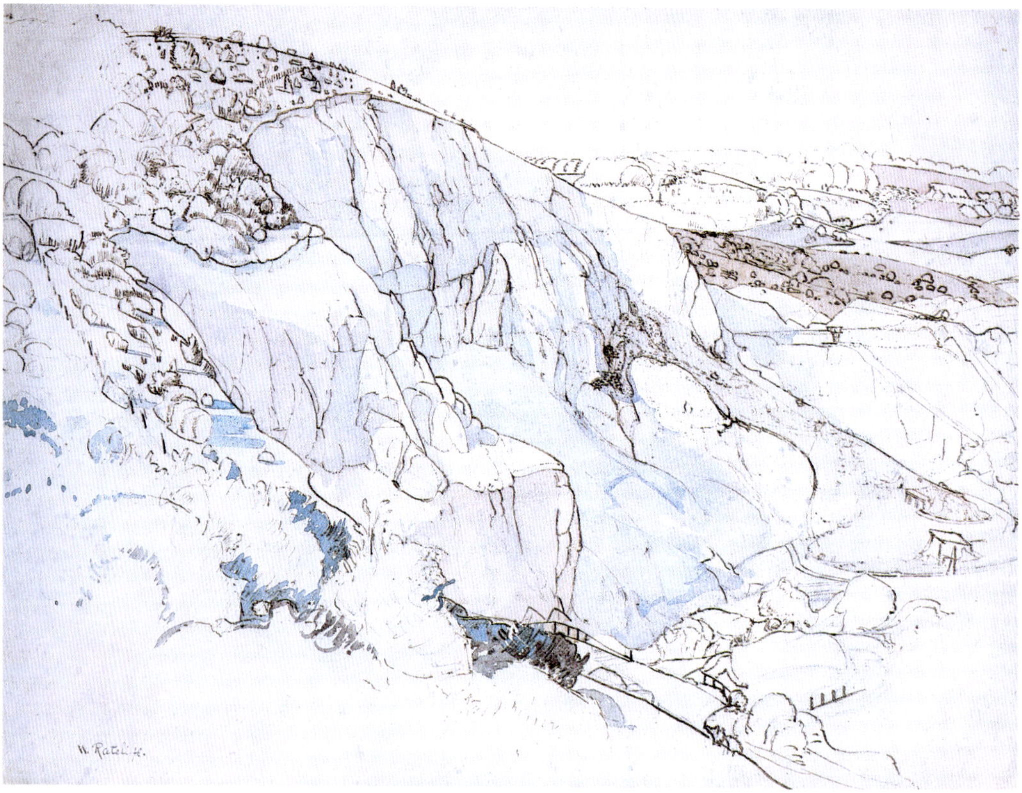

WILLIAM RATCLIFFE
Rocks, Cornwall, ca. 1920s
Ink and watercolour,
405 x 542 mm
Southampton City Art Gallery

Bohemian, almost itinerant existence, but he became still more transient in his later years as his fortunes diminished. From 1916 he became increasingly dependant on his brother S.K. Ratcliffe, with whom he lived for many years in various locations, including Berkhamsted and Whiteley in the Chilterns. His brother once suggested that he might make some money by painting scenes of Boston, Lincolnshire, to sell in Boston, USA, and he tried it; but it was not a success, even though Ratcliffe exhibited work both in Boston and at the Art Institute of Chicago.

Around 1930 Ratcliffe moved back to Letchworth, and from 1937 to 1946 he rented a flat in the High Street in nearby Baldock, before returning to live with the Parkers at Wilbury Road, Letchworth. Almost constantly on the move, with most of his possessions fitting in a rucksack and his easel and paintbox also portable, he often stayed with kind friends, one of whom reported that he was an inexpensive guest since he ate little – mostly cornflakes.[24]

In 1946 the Roland Browse and Delbanco Galleries staged Ratcliffe's first one-man show in London. Since none of the oil paintings exhibited there was made after 1921 it has been supposed that he gave up oils at that date. Certainly the quality and confidence of the design of his painting declined markedly after 1914, and he may simply have been unable to afford oil paint. He transferred his attention to ink and watercolour, and also wood engraving, and here he enjoyed a renaissance. As a body of work his drawings and watercolours manifest carefully observed and accurate draftsmanship, an eye for detail, and delicate coloration. Despite the obvious merits of his work Ratcliffe sold very little during his lifetime. Instead he gave much of it away as gifts to his friends, in lieu of keep. His dentist in Belsize Park reputedly had a number of his paintings![25]

Letchworth Museum and Art Gallery hold photographs of Ratcliffe helping to install his paintings at an exhibition held there in August 1954. That must have been his last public appearance, for his health soon deteriorated and he departed to spend his remaining months with relatives in Hampstead. He died in January 1955, aged eighty-four, in obscurity. Yet Ratcliffe deserves a place in art history, albeit modest. He was part of the dynamic and significant movement which effectively launched British modernism, and at the height of his powers in 1913 he was making work nearly comparable in stature to Gilman's. Had Ratcliffe not met Harold Gilman, his life and art would surely have followed a quite different course.

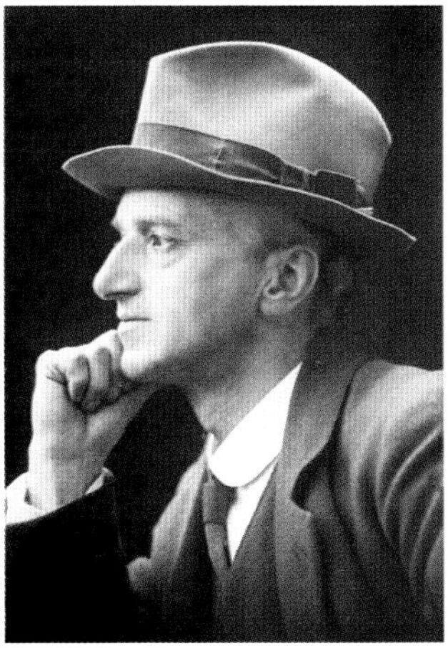

WILLIAM RATCLIFFE

POSTSCRIPT A private lender to this exhibition has written to the author with a personal recollection of the artist: "I well remember visiting William Ratcliffe with my father before the war – probably in 1936 when I was 9 years old [....] Ratcliffe then lived in an attic in 35 Whitehorse Street in Baldock – on the Great North Road in fact. The attic overlooked an antique tiled shed – 'the barn' – which Ratcliffe sketched. Ratcliffe's attic had a low ceiling and only one window, a semi-circular Diocletian window, overlooking 'the barn'. The visit is strangely fixed in my memory. The room was very sparely furnished: a bed, the painter's paraphernalia – easel, pots of brushes, and a Victorian washstand with a white marble top on which stood a jug and basin and a very large tube of Chrome Yellow oil paint – clearly labelled. William Ratcliffe boiled a kettle on a gas ring and made tea. My father and William Ratcliffe sat in the two chairs and I sat on the bed."[26]

NOTES

1. Walter Bayes, 'The Camden Town Group', *Saturday Review*, 25 January 1930; quoted Wendy Baron, *Perfect Moderns: A History of the Camden Town Group*, London (Ashgate) 2000, p. 44.

2. 'Idealism', *Art News*, 12 May 1910; ibid., p. 29.

3. *Letchworth, The World's First Garden City*, Letchworth (North Hertfordshire District Council and Letchworth Garden City Corporation), n.d. [*ca.* 2000].

4. Wendy Baron, *Miss Ethel Sands and her Circle*, London (Peter Owen) 1977; Baron, cit. note 1, pp. 24 and 25.

5. Barbara Duce (the artist's niece), letter to the author, 2002.

6. Ibid.

7. Baron, cit. note 1, p. 34.

8. Ibid., p. 44.

9. Barbara Duce, cit. note 5.

10. Andrew Causey, 'Harold Gilman: An Englishman and Post-Impressionism', in *Harold Gilman, 1876–1919*, exhib. cat., Arts Council of Great Britain, 1981, p. 11.

11. Note by Martin Brunt on a conversation with Timothy Hinton, Stanley Parker's grandson, 1991.

12. Walter Sickert, in *The New Age*, 2 June 1910; Baron, cit. note 1, p. 32.

13. Ibid., p. 72.

14. P. Wyndham Lewis and L.F. Ferguson, *Harold Gilman: An Appreciation*, London (Chatto & Windus) 1919, p. 13; Baron, cit. note 1, p. 42.

15. Ibid., p. 70.

16. Ibid.

17. Hubert Wellington, in *Charles Ginner. 1878–1952*, exhib. cat., Arts Council, 1953.

18. Baron, cit. note 1, p. 72.

19. *The New Age*, 25 June 1914.

20. Causey, cit. note 10, p. 16.

21. *The Painters of Camden Town 1905–1920*, exhib. cat., Christie's, London, January 1988, p. 163.

22. Julian Agnew, introduction, *Harold Gilman 1876-1919: An English Post-Impressionist*, exhib. cat., The Minories, Colchester, 1969.

23. Southampton City Art Gallery archive.

24. *William Ratcliffe*, exhib. cat., Letchworth Museum and Art Gallery, 1982, p. 10.

25. Ibid.

26. Martin Brunt, letter to the author, 2002.

"... a clean and solid mosaic ...": Harold Gilman and William Ratcliffe was first published to accompany an exhibition at Southampton City Art Gallery, 26 April –7 July 2002.

Southampton City Art Gallery
Civic Centre
Southampton SO14 7LP
Tel + 44 (0)23 8083 2277
Fax + 44 (0) 23 8083 2153
art.gallery@southampton.gov.uk

Southampton City Art Gallery staff: Charlotte Baber, Sheila Belson, Pat Cobb, Colin Cobbold, Tim Craven, Les Crook, Jan Davies, Emily Dickinson, Ray Hurst, Vicky Isley, John Lawrence, David Lawton, Christopher Locke, Esta Mion-Jones, Rebecca Moisan, Brian Mortimer, Denis Stevens
with thanks to Ros Allwood, Monica Beck, Adrian Hunt, Clare Mitchell, Ambrose Scott-Moncrief, Rosie Shirley, Godfrey Worsdale

Published by order of Southampton City Art Gallery, 2002

ISBN 1 903470 03 X

Designed by Roger Davies
daviesdesign@onetel.net.uk
www.rogerdaviesdesign.co.uk

Produced by
Paul Holberton publishing,
37 Snowsfields, London SE1 4QG
books@paul-holberton.demon.co.uk

Printed in Italy